Gospel & Culture in North East India

Christian Heritage Rediscovered

The Series, as the name suggests, is meant to focus on Christian Faith & Living vis-à-vis topics like Literature & Poetry, Indigenous Philosophizing, Ethical response towards Agriculture, Health & Healing, Science & Technology, Eco-feminist Theology, Sociological approach towards Human Rights, Law & Politics, Arts, History of Ideas, Ancient Civilizations, Cultural Contiguity, Religious Cosmologies & Mysticism, Footsteps of famous Theologians, World Peace & Harmony, Global Capitalism, Network Marketing, Cybertheology, Population & Demographics, Epigraphic Studies, Contextualized Education, and many others. We welcome a Mss. on any topic/s mentioned, whether they are original works, scholarly monographs, collections of conference papers, revised dissertations, or translations of historical documents. Through the Series we, the Publishers, are striving to put forward published works that may help Institutions, Academic Bodies, Researchers, Scholars and the World at large in furthering their respective knowledge and understanding on the concerned subject. We welcome your comments on our efforts and further suggestions on how we can foster the upcoming thought provoking theologically grounded books.

Christian Heritage Rediscovered - 73

Gospel & Culture in North East India

A Missiological & Anthropological Study from Zeliangrong Perspective

Rampaukube Hekwet

CWI

Christian World Imprints

First Published in 2019 by

Christian World Imprints
Christian Publishing & Books from India
H-12 Bali Nagar, **New Delhi-110015**
info@christianworldimprints.com
www.ChristianWorldImprints.com
Phone: +91 11 25465925

ISBN: 978-93-5148-334-2 (HB)
ISBN: 978-93-5148-335-9 (PB)

Printed in India.

CONTENTS

This book in its original form is the thesis submitted to the Senate of Serampore College (University), India, towards the degree of Master of Theology (M. Th.) and is published with the written permission. The author is responsible for the title, contents and opinions in it.

The original title of the thesis is "A Missiological Study of the Encounter between Christianity and Zeliangrong Culture" but for the purpose of publication the title is reconstructed and the content is revised to the present form.

DEDICATION

This humble work is dedicated to my loving parents
Mr. Ileuheing (late) and Ms. Ikiebamle, who brought me up,
taught and encouraged me to love and serve the Lord like them.

FOREWORD-I

Any mission engagement has to ask itself certain important questions: Is mission engagement primarily about changing the adherence of people from one religion to another? Is mission engagement also concerned with changing the culture of the people? Is the objective of mission engagement to change the identity, faith, culture and life-style of the people to make the same match the identity, faith, culture and life-style of the missionaries? A reading of Rampaukube Hekwet's book ***Gospel and Culture in North East India: A Missiological & Anthropological Study from Zeliangrong Perspective*** raises these very questions about mission engagements.

One is reminded of the famous work of H. Richard Niebuhr, *Christ and Culture*, published in 1915 in which he presented five prevailing view-points on the subject:

*Christ against Culture***:** This first perspective encourages opposition, total separation, and hostility toward culture, and a commitment to create a separate, pure community (that is, culture) of Christians.

Christ of Culture: This second viewpoint is exactly the opposite of "Christ against Culture" because it attempts to bring culture and Christianity together, regardless of their differences. Liberation, process, and feminist theologies are recent examples.

Christ above Culture: This third position, as Donald Bloesch puts it, attempts "to correlate the fundamental questions of the culture with the answer of Christian revelation." Thomas Aquinas is the most prominent teacher of this viewpoint.

Christ and Culture in Paradox: According to this perspective, the Christian belongs "to two realms (the spiritual and temporal) and must live in the tension of fulfilling responsibilities to both." Martin Luther adopted this view.

Christ Transforming Culture: The fifth position highlights the attempt to convert the values and goals of secular culture into the service of the kingdom of God.

In many cases of missiological engagement, the focus is on relating the religion and culture of a people to a person, Jesus Christ. However, we need to keep in mind that Jesus Christ himself related his life and work to the reign of God in the context of the people: "The Spirit of the Lord is upon me, because he has anointed me to bring good news to the poor. He has sent me to proclaim release to the captives and recovery of sight to the blind, to let the oppressed go free, and to proclaim the year of the Lord's favor."

Therefore in Missiology, as Hekwet seeks to impress upon us, we should see the relevance of the gospel of Jesus Christ to the context of the people. The Gospel should be one that liberates people from unjust and unwholesome systems, structures, and practices, while at the same time facilitating the dignified and holistic growth of individuals and the community within their political, socio-economic, and religio-cultural contexts. The gospel celebrates the solidarity and fellowship of a plurality of peoples with their respective races, ethnicities, and ways of life, committed to and giving expression to the values of justice, love and peace, indeed the reign of God.

Rev. Dr. Roger Gaikwad
General Secretary
National Council of Churches in India
23rd May, 2018

FOREWORD-II

This book ***Gospel and Culture in North East India: A Missiological & Anthropological Study from Zeliangrong Perspective*** by Rampaukube Hekwet is a historical research on the traditional customs and culture of Zeliangrong Naga people in North East India. The author Hekwet, is a Mission student who made a serious enquiry on the pre Christian era cultural life of Zeliangrong people. He gave good introduction to the Zeliangrong people, with respect to their geographical location, origin and migration to the present settlements. He dealt extensively on the socio-political life, domestic life, economic life, leisure and recreation, law and customs, worldviews, religious practices, Social and religious festivals and value systems of the Zeliangrong people.

He discussed on how Christianity came to Zeliangrong people and makes impact on the culture and brought drastic changes in their lives. At the same time, the author also candidly portraits the clash, confusion, tensions and irrelevancy of the Gospel and the culture in the process of encountering with each other. The Christian mission came along with colonialism and presented western culture as the only God ordained, valid and normative means for living, considering the culture of the people as primitive and anti-Christian. The people saw the foreignness of the Christian message to their culture therefore, opposed and resisted to the coming of the Christianity to Zeliangrong Naga territory till today in the form of Heraka and Tingkao Raguang traditional Religious sects.

The Zeliangrong Baptist Church history was extensively researched and presented as to how the Zeliangrong people embraced Christianity as their newfound faith in Jesus Christ. The process of evangelism and the growth and maturity of new believers in Christ were carefully documented. The outpouring of the Holy Spirit and the Revival movement in the Zeliangrong churches was mentioned. The formation of Zeliangrong Baptist Churches Association and the reasons and process of segregation into Zeme Baptist Association Nsong, Liangmai Baptist Association Tening, The Rongmei Baptist Association Jalukie, The Zeme Baptist Association Jalukie and the Zeme Baptist Church Council Peren were carefully observed and described. Besides, the emergence and existences of different denominational groups such as Roman Catholic, Christian Revival, Presbyterian, Seventh Day Adventist, Pentecostal, and Independent church was also acknowledged.

Critical analysis was done on how the Christian faith has impacted and made its influence on Zeliangrong culture. The negative outcomes and positive impact of the Christian Faith in the process of encountering with Zeliangrong culture were evaluated. The continuity and residues of Cultural elements in the churches and Christian day today living is observed and discussed. The continuous tension and clash between Christian faith and Zeliangrong culture in existence is notified.

The author gave some concrete suggestions and recommendations as to how the Zeliangrong churches can participate in the mission of God more seriously and effectively with the involvement of youths, women, laity, and the whole church as missionary force. He emphasizes on the Spirit filled mission, unity in mission, partnership in mission, and holistic mission. Suggestion was given to restructure the existing mission structures for better achievement and result.

This book is the newest reflections on the Zeliangrong culture and Christian faith, written from a missiological perspective and attempted to show how best the gospel can be relevantly presented in the given cultural context. It bears some of the Anthropological and Missiological principles to bear in mind in gospel presentation, to be acceptable and relevant to any given culture. This is a solid information piece of Zeliangrong Christianity and Culture.

I strongly recommend this book to all the Zeliangrong Christian Leaders, Pastors, Mission leaders, Theological students, Researchers and lay people who want to know more about our Zeliangrong history, traditions and culture. This book will be of a great help.

Rev. Dr. Rabi Pame
Director, Blessing Ministry
Dimapur, Nagaland
13th June, 2018

ACKNOWLEDGMENTS

This research work has been accomplished through the invaluable help I received from many individuals, institutions and organizations, thus, I would like to sincerely acknowledge them.

I sincerely express my profound gratitude to Prof. Dr. Roger Gaikwad, my mentor, for shaping my thoughts with his invaluable guidance and encouragement throughout the research work and for the beautiful foreword. I am deeply indebted to him. I also would like to sincerely express my thanks to Rev. Dr. Rabi Pame, Director, Blessing Ministry, Dimapur, who is also the Principal of United College of Theology and Mission (UCTM) for beautifully penning down the another foreword to the book. I also express my sincere gratitude to Joanna Heat (Renthlei) for patiently proofreading my manuscript.

My heartfelt thanks and gratitude also goes to Synod Theological Education Board of Mizoram Presbyterian Church for sponsoring my studies at the Aizawl Theological College. I sincerely express my profound thanks to the Zeme Baptist Church Council Peren for the grant of Stipend Scholarship and my beloved parents and well wishers for moral support and financial assistance towards my studies and research.

My sincere thanks and appreciations are due also to the library staff of ATC Aizawl and ETC Jorhat, and leaders of ZBCC, ZBA, LBA and RBA for allowing me to use their resources and all my interviewees and respondents to my questionnaire for providing me resources for the study.

I am deeply indebted to Christian World Imprints, New Delhi, for publishing this book.

Finally, I am extremely grateful to all my beloved family members who always remain supportive to my studies and ministry, especially Azaile, my wife, for lovingly and faithfully supporting me.

Above all glory and honor be to God, who is my help and strength.

Rampaukube Hekwet
Aizawl, 15th June, 2018

INTRODUCTION

1. The Problem

The Zeliangrong Christian identity evolved out of the encounter between Christian mission and the Zeliangrong Naga culture, leading to confusion of identity, thereby exposing some failures in the Christian mission. This necessitates a study to analyze that encounter from a missiological perspective. The Zeliangrong people had received the gospel in the last decade of the 19th century. Since then, there was a tremendous growth of the church in the Zeliangrong area, through the effort of the Christian missionaries and the local churches. Thus, the encounter between Christian mission and the Zeliangrong culture took place. This encounter has had a significant impact on both the Zeliangrong people of other faiths and the Zeliangrong Christians. The Christian mission that came along with western imperialism on one hand seems to have presented the missionaries' western culture as God-ordained, in contrast to the native culture and traditional way of life which was perceived as primitive, dirty and anti-Christian. Sadly, the people seem to have responded obediently to this imposition, considering western Christianity as normative, with no critical assessment. As a result, Christians were accused by the traditional believers of devaluing and abandoning their own culture. On the other hand, though the Zeliangrong people responded to the Christian mission and became Christians, there is still an observable cultural continuity.

Consequently, a new identity came into being for the Zeliangrong Nagas as Zeliangrong Christians.

Today, the Christian mission appears to be making less progress than before, as it is not ingrained in the culture of the people, and as the western culture is not the inherent culture locally. Thus, it weakens the eventual outcome of the mission works of the Church. Besides, the mission work now seems to be not very relevant for the people. Therefore, the researcher seeks to engage in an attempt at provoking the consciousness of the churches, missionaries and Christians in general, to revitalize the healthy cultural values and integrate these in the mission strategy which may be effective, and culturally and contextually relevant for mission work.

2. Scope and Limitation

The Zeliangrong Nagas live in three major districts of North East India, viz., Assam, Manipur and Nagaland; and it is difficult to cover the whole geographical area due to the time limit for the research. Therefore, the writer limits the study geographically only to Peren District in Nagaland, as the Zeliangrong people predominantly live here. The study also confines itself ecclesiastically to the Baptist denominational group as they represent the majority of the Zeliangrong Christians, and chooses to confine itself to the domain of cultural influence on the Zeliangrong Christians as this has not been widely addressed in other work.

3. Previous Works

As far as the topic is concerned, studies on the impact of the Christian mission on the Zeliangrong culture have been done before,[1] but other researchers did not make any attempt to study the cultural

[1] Pamei Ramkhun, *The Zeliangrong Nagas: A Study of Tribal Christianity* (New Delhi: Uppal Publishing House, 1996)., Namthiubuiyang Pamei, *The Trial from Makuilongdi: The Continuing Saga of the Zeliangrong People,* (Tamenglong: Gironto Charitable Foundation, 2001)., Haisuitei, "A Historical Study of Christianity and Heraka Cult Among Zeliangrong People of Nagaland" (B. D. thesis, United Theological College, Bangalore, 1989., Namnabi Hegui, "A study of the Customary Laws of the Zeliangrong Nagas" (B. D. Thesis, Eastern Theological College, Jorhat, 1994).

influence on Christianity in the encounter between the Zeliangrong culture and the Christian mission. Therefore, this is a new area of study and poses a great challenge.

4. Method of Research

This study basically employs an analytical method to find out the impact of Christianity on culture and vice-versa in forming a distinctive Christian identity. It also takes up a historical approach and empirical method by which the authenticity of the historical sources will be examined and the pragmatic experiential situation of the impact on each other is assessed. The study tries to employ some of Richard Niebuhr's five propositions of *Christ and Culture* as far as applicable as an analytical tool.

5. Structure

The first chapter introduces who the Zeliangrong are; their origin, their land, and their socio-political, cultural and religious background. The second chapter deals with the dawn of Christianity, the opposition from the traditional society, and the formation and division of the Baptist Associations. It also highlights the presence of other denominational traditions. The third chapter studies the encounter between Christianity and the Zeliangrong traditional culture and evaluates the outcome of the encounter; the revival movement which has significant impact on the life of the Christian is discussed, and the cultural continuity among the Christians today is traced. The fourth chapter discusses the present state of Christianity and the attitude of Zeliangrong Christians to their culture. The mission works of the four associations are evaluated and assessed. The fifth and final chapter looks at critical issues in mission strategy for relevant and effective mission.

Chapter 1

THE ZELIANGRONG NAGAS AND THEIR LAND

Introduction

The Zeliangrong people are a distinct Naga tribe, having many similarities with other Naga tribes as well as having their own unique entity. To know them, one has to look into their socio, economic, political and religious life. Therefore, this chapter traces the past lives of the Zeliangrong people, examining who and what kind of people they are, where they come from and how they have attained their present status, their thought forms and their value systems.

1.1. Zeliangrong and their habitation

1.1.1. The home of the Zeliangrong

The Zeliangrong Nagas have been living in their present habitation since time immemorial. They live in a geographically contiguous region in the states of North East India (NEI), along the Barrail Mountain and its southern ranges, viz., Assam, Manipur and Nagaland.[1] The total area of land inhabited is estimated to be

[1] Achung Xavier Longmei, "Zeliangrong Movement: A search for Identity," *Souvenir: North East India Zeliangrong Naga Festival-Cum Seminar* (Imphal: Literature and Souvenir Committee. NEIZNFS, 1995), 10. Hereafter, Achung

about 12,000 sq. kms. The integral land of the Zeliangrongs was dissected by the British into three separate political units in 1930s for administrative convenience and political expediency.[2] As a result, the Zeliangrong Nagas were placed in three different states, making them minority groups in those states, thus weakening the unity of a people who had once been the first people in the Naga Hills who fought against the British under the leadership of *Jadonang* and *Rani Gaidinliu* as early as 1927.[3]

1.1.2. Peren District

The area of study is confined mainly to *Peren* District. It is a mountainous terrain encompassing fertile foothill valley plains in the North-West and North-East. It occupies the lengthened South-western end of Nagaland, located between longitude 93°E-94°E and latitude 25°N-26°N of the equator. It is about 2300 sq. kms in size and shares boundaries with Manipur state in the South and East, with Assam in the west, with *Dimapur* district on its North and with *Kohima* district on its North-East. Its elevation varies from 800 mts. to 2500 mts. above sea level. There are 85 recognised villages, 10 unrecognized villages, three major towns and three small towns. According to the 2001 census, the population was 96,825 of which 50,001 were male and 46,823 female. The literacy rate of the district exceeds 54% of which 32% are male and 22% are female. The Christian population is approximately 95% of the total population.[4] It has a monsoon type of climate with cold winters and

---

Xavier, *Zeliangrong Movement…,* Particularly in Peren District of Nagaland, North Cachar Hills sub-division of Assam and Tamenglong, Sadar Hills sub-division of Senapati district, northern portion of Henglep sub-division of Churachanpur district and Jiribam sub-division of Imphal district in Manipur.

[2] Gonreipou Kamei, "Road Transport system in Zeliangrong Areas in North East India," *Souvenir: North East India Zeliangrong Naga Festival-Cum Seminar* (Imphal: Literature and Souvenir Committee. NEIZNFS, 1995), 24.

[3] G. Makuga, *Introduction to the Rongmei Nagas* (Imphal: Mr & Mrs Makuga, 1994), 125. Hereafter, Makuga, *Introduction to the Rongmei…*

[4] Peren District, Profile in Commemoration of Peren District Inauguration, 11th February, 2004. 1-2, 11. Hereafter, Peren, *Profile…,* Mt. Paona is the highest mountain peak in the district at 2500 mts. high and Peren Town, the Headquarter is 1445.40 mts. above sea level.

mild summers. It has an annual rainfall of 1500 mm. to 3000 mm. during the months of July to September.[5]

1.1.3. Origin of the Zeliangrong

The Zeliangrong tribe is one of the major Naga tribes of the NEI. In the tribal countryside of the NEI, the Zeliangrong people are a distinctive model of the fruition of a common identity of a group of cognate tribes who were, though of common origin, divided by a hostile geography and external power in history, followed by social non-communication and lack of common organization. But they are united by certain common bonds such as common origin, affinity and cultural heritage, armored by common experiences of exploitation from alien assailants.

1.1.4. The term Zeliangrong

The British administrators bisected the Zeliangrong people into various names, such as 'Kacha Naga' for the Zeme and Liangmai and 'Kabui' for the Rongmei in Manipur, Zeliang in Nagaland and Zeme in Assam.[6] However, the cognate tribes of Zeme, Liangmai and Rongmei have a common ancestry; having known their kinship they formed their nomenclature by taking the prefix of each tribes as Ze+Liang+Rong= Zeliangrong on the 15th February 1947 at Keishamthong, Imphal, so that they now represent all the three kin tribes.[7] The affinity of the Zeliangrong people is proven by their traditions and customs such as songs, folklore, attire and dances.

---

5 Peren, Profile…, 4, 5. The mean annual temperature in the hill sector ranges from 18° Celsius to 26°C and in the valley sector, from 18°C to 35°C. The mean December and January temperature in the hill sector ranges from 2°C-4°C to 10°C-15°C and in the valley sector ranges from 10°C-20°C.

6 Sipra Sen, *The Tribes and Castes of Manipur* (New Delhi: Mittal Publications, 1992), 52. Hereafter, Sipra, *The Tribes….*

7 Namthiubuiyang Pamei, *The Trial from Makuilongdi: The Continuing Saga of the Zeliangrong People* (Tamenglong: Gironta Charitable Foundation, 2001), 51. Hereafter, Namthiubuiyang, *The Trial from Makuilongdi….*

1.1.5. Origin and Migration

The Zeliangrong People have a very strong awareness of the past but it is a mixture of myths, legends and traditions preserved in their ritual hymns, their songs and oral traditions. The Zeliangrong Nagas have an obscured theory of origin. Therefore, there cannot be a concrete and proven theory about it. Their traditional belief is that the ancestors came out of a mythical cave called *taobei*.[8] They undoubtedly belong to the Mongoloid race and R. R. Shimray might be right in agreeing with Marshall and locating the Naga origin to somewhere in South East Asia.[9] Later on, the Zeliangrong Nagas along with other Nagas came to Makhel, now a Mao Naga village in North Manipur.[10] It appeared that from Makhel the ancestors of the Zeliangrong Nagas moved southward where they reached Ramting Kabin and they made another move until they finally came and settled at Makuilongdi near the present Oklong village.[11] The Zeliangrong people prospered and populated in this village and their number of houses according to the tradition reached the mark of 7,777. As the population continued to expand, perhaps due to shortage of land for cultivation, they again migrated from Makuilongdi to their present places of habitation.[12]

---

[8] Ramkhun Pamei, *The Zeliangrong Nagas: A study of Tribal Christianity,* (New Delhi: Uppal Publishing House, 1996), 6. Hereafter, Ramkhun, *The Zeliangrong…,* Taobei no longer seems to exist today.

[9] R. R. Shimray, *Origin and Culture of Nagas* (New Delhi: Pamleiphi, 1985), 12-13. Hereafter, R. R. Shimray, *Origin and Culture….* The version holds that the early home of the peoples of Asia was in the upper reaches of the Huangho/ Yellow River of China and from this centre the early tribes of Indo-China moved to southward.

[10] M. Hussain, *Nagaland, Encycloopedia of India, Vol. XIX* (New Delhi: Rima Publishing House, 1994), 26. Which was a point of dispersal in the story of migration of the Naga tribes, this village is about 38 kilometers away from Kohima, the capital of Nagaland.

[11] See Namthiubuiyang, *The Trial from Makuilongdi…,* 14; Ramkhun, *The Zeliangrong…,* 6. Here they led a settled life based on shifting agriculture, therefore this place is considered as the cradle of the Zeliangrong cultures and customs.

12 Ramkhun, The Zeliangrong…, 6, 7. There are a number of traditions about the dispersions of the Zeliangrong people from Makuilongdi, the most two probable theories are given here. The first holds that a group of migrants went to the

1.2. Socio-political and Cultural life

The Zeliangrong social life is grounded in the family, clan, *morung* and village. The Zeliangrong society is a patriarchal society. The value of public social life is stronger than that of individuals in the society.

1.2.1. Marriage and Family

The Zeliangrong people have two kinds of marriage; *Hengyi meu,* which is conducted during the festival season, is a holy marriage, and *Hekak meu* is conducted in any season of the year.[13] Generally the Zeme have small families consisting of the father, mother and the unmarried children, but in the case of the Liangmai and the Rongmei they practice joint family system where the married couples live with their children, parents and unmarried brothers and sisters.[14] The father in both cases is the head and priest of the family. The properties are inherited by the sons. They practice clan exogamy in marriage.

---

northern and western slopes of the great Barail range in search of plains; they came to be known as Zeme or the dwellers of the plain and hot land. Another group went towards the south which was an unoccupied barren land of the southern direction and inhabitants of the maruong vacant land; they were latter known as Maruongmei which was corrupted to Rongmei. Those who remain back at Makuilongdi and in the nearby areas were latter known as Liangmai, the northerners. The second tradition says that Nguiba was the chief of Makuilongdi, he had no heir. Knowing that there will be none to inherit him, the villagers brought another girl for him, so he had two wives. His second wife borne him a son named Nrimbangbe who became the father of the Liangmai, then the first wife also borne him two sons. The first of the two was named as Namregang who become the progenitor of the Zeme and the younger son was called Kading who became the father of the Rongmei. Looking at the above discussion one can be certain that the Zeliangrong people share the kinship relationship with each other. Their attachment to Makuilongdi from wherever they came to their present country cannot be easily overlooked.

[13] Heisuiding Irangbe, Teiheilung Kulimbe, *Benreu Paupai Rennet Ha Laisiukwak* (Dimapur: Paupai Renet me Nkwah Benreu, 2004), 19. Hereafter, Heisuiding, *Benreu Paupai Renet....*

[14] Ramkhun, *The Zeliangrong...,* 28. The joint family system is practiced because of their love for parents. However it is not compulsory, the choice is left to the couple to either remain or separate.

1.2.2. Clan

The Zeliangrong society is a patriarchal society with two moiety or major clans, namely; *Pame* and *Newme* or *Hau* and *Heu* which are further subdivided into many exogamous clans and sub-clans. These two major clans are found in all the three cognate tribes which are subdivided into different clans with different names.[15] This unit is made up of several families related by blood. M. Horam has rightly said that, "any clan can be traced back to a single family which has multiplied into numerous families but remain connected to each other."[16]

1.2.3. *Hangsiuki*

The term *Hangsiuki* means house of the bachelors or male dormitory. Joseph S. Thong called it a men's club.[17] It was usually the house of a respectable man within the clan. *Hangsiuki* was prominent in most of the Zeliangrong villages; the state of *Hangsiuki* indicated the state of the village itself.[18] The *hangsiuki* were administered by the senior members at the advice of the elders and "Obedience and discipline were the watch words."[19] *Hangsiuki* had an immense impact on the Zeliangrong people as it socialized the citizens. It was the centre of the Zeliangrong social life, where young boys were trained, disciplined and given instructions on moral principles of self-denial and obedience for the cause of the society. Primarily *hangsiuki* ensured security and peace to the community.[20]

---

[15] Ramkhun, *The Zeliangrong...*, 5.

[16] M. Horam, *Social and Cultural Life of Naga: The Thangkhul Nagas* (Delhi: B. R. Publishing Corporation, 1977), 62-63.

[17] Joseph S. Thong, *Head-hunters Culture: Historic Culture of Nagas* (Chunlika Tsemenyu: Khinyi Woch, 1997), 87.

[18] Verrier Elwin, *Nagaland* (Shillong: P. Dutta for Research Department, 1961), 75. Hereafter, Verrier, *Nagaland*...Thus, *Hangsiuki* were well kept and decorated with skulls and war trophies, and the pillars were carved with striking representations of tigers, hornbills, human figures, elephants and mithuns.

[19] R. R. Shimray, *Origin and Culture...*, 194.

[20] See Heisuiding, Benreu Paupai Renet ..., 28; K. Thanzauva, *Theology of Community: Tribal Theology in the Making* (Aizawl: Mizo Theological Conference, 1997), 137. Hereafter, Thanzauva, Theology.... The young men kept vigil and guarded the village both day and night, as the tribal life in the past was insecure

It also served as a forum and an information center for the villagers as well as a protective sanctuary, since no criminal could be touched while in *hangsiuki*.[21]

The counterpart of *hangsiuki* was the girls' dormitory which was called *Releiki* or *leiseuki. Releiki* served as a learning centre in the past; the girls were trained how to love one another, share and cooperate; singing, weaving and stitching were taught there.[22] They simultaneously disciplined themselves for shouldering motherly responsibilities in the future.[23]

1.2.4. Village

The village is the primary social and political institution for the Zeliangrong Nagas. The Zeliangrong villages are usually set on hill tops, in a strategic place for their war and safety because they also practiced headhunting.[24] The villages were founded with strict rules of the customary laws. They have a strong attachment to their villages and lands.[25] The form of government differed from village to village, ranging from monarchical to democratic forms of government.[26] The practice of chieftainship, *Hegwang,* among the Zeliangrong

---

because of the practice of head-hunting.Emergency times like in the case of sickness or death in distant places away from home were also a time for vigilance.

[21] This is because the men of the *hangsiuki* would at all costs protect him till the case had been settled. Besides, certain religious rites were performed. Therefore, it was a sanctuary sacred and holy in its own way for the people.

[22] Elungkiebe Zeliang,"The Socio-Economic and Political History of Zeliangrong Naga" (B.D. thesis, Eastern Theological college, 1996). Hereafter, Elungkiebe, *The Socio-Economic....*

[23] H. Bareh, ed., *Gazzeetter of India-Nagaland: Kohima District* (Kohima: Government of Nagaland, 1970), 85. Hereafter, Bareh, *Gazzeetter of India...*

[24] Robert Reid, *History of the Frontier Areas Bordering of/on Assam 1883-1941*, (Delhi: Eastern Publishing House, first Publish, 1942), 1983, 81.

[25] Ramkhun, *The Zeliangrong...*, 24.

[26] See Achung Xavier, *Zeliangrong Movement...*, 10; Elungkiebe, *The Socio-Economic...*56. Many of the villages have a village chief called *Hegwang* meaning king, who administered the government with his councilors. On the other hand, some villages have no chief as such but only the village councilors called *Hangkiame or Peikai* who administered the village government.

people must have originated when they were at *Chawangpungning.*[27] Normally for the Zeme, a few families belonging to two different major clans, i.e., *Heu* and *Hau* formed groups and established new villages, in which the most able member of the first clan became the chief and the most able man from the second clan became the priest of the village.[28] The Zeliangrong *Hegwang* system therefore had dual functions, viz., political and religious.[29]

1.2.5. Food, drinks, ornaments, songs and dances

Rice is the stable food supplemented by other vegetables and meats. Rice beer is the essential ingredient of their everyday drink.[30] The Zeliangrong sense of protocol can be seen in the clothes and shawls they wear. They have numerous types with different designs for men and women according to different age groups. They highly favor colorful ornaments like ivory, carnelian beads, iron and other fineries. During ceremonial occasions they appeared like royal dignitaries.[31] Songs and dances played an important role in the life of the Zeliangrong people; they still love singing and dancing together in groups. Their songs lighten their daily course of work. The songs varied according to festival, work, war, and sacrifice; for all occasions they had songs to be sung individually or in groups.[32]

---

[27] Namthiubuiyang, *The Trial from Makuilongdi...*, 9. This is one of the places where their ancestors were supposed to have settled once in the past.

[28] Rampaukube Hekwet, "Analytical Study of the Zeliangrong Naga Traditional Ethical Values and Its implications for a Just Society" (B.D. thesis, Senate of Serampore College, 2004).

[29] Firstly, as secular head he was responsible for the defense of the village; peace and prosperity also depended on the ability of the chief, the chief also played a vital role in the judicial matters with his councilors. Secondly, as religious priest he also performed some religious rites.

[30] Every household prepared and stored the drink in a big wooden drum and several gourd vessels. It is a nourishing drink for them as they are hard working people thus they drink rice beer called *zautau* for energizing themselves.

[31] Ramkhun, *The Zeliangrong Nagas...*, 26, 27. They adorn themselves with head-gear, horn-bill feathers, grand shawls with necklaces and earrings which make them look regal.

[32] Ramkhun, *The Zeliangrong Nagas...*, 25.

1.3. Economic life

Their economic life has depended on their labor and resources. They were self-dependent, hard-working and produced their own essential commodities. Their community spirit was strongly seen in their economic co-existence in the sense that they had a strong feeling towards helping and taking care of others' needs. That is why among the Zeliangrong Nagas begging is not seen. Agriculture was the main occupation in the early days; they adopted the jhum system or shifting cultivation.[33]

They also practiced terraced fields, which are of two kinds; the dry terrace called *Langkie-luu*, and the wet terrace called *Dui-luu or redei.*[34] In the terrace fields they grow paddy and other vegetables. Besides these, snails and fishes for consumption are found in large quantity. The terrace fields are permanent fields and it is prestigious to own huge wet terrace fields.

Besides cultivation, they domesticate animals.[35] They also depend on the forest resources; tea is grown and is one of the important products of their land and a source of income.[36] They depend also on their artistic works; by nature many of their males are skillful in different professions, like wood carving, crafting and blacksmithing, and their females engage in spinning, weaving and pottery. They also manufacture *caitei* (salt) in their traditional way by extracting it

---

[33] They go to hills, clear the jungles, burn patches of land, plant paddy and other vegetables. In the next year they go to another place. Thus there is a rotation of cultivation over the course of eight to ten years.

[34] B. C. Allen, et.al., eds., *Gazetter of Bengal and the North East India* (Delhi: Mittal Publications, 1976), 63. Hereafter, Allen *Gazetter*.... Dry terraces have water only in seasons, while wet terraces have water all through the year. These kinds of fields are maintained with proper irrigation systems and the channels are designed to distribute water over each terrace in series. Forest resources like timbers, bamboo, canes, cinnamon, stones, agur, myrrh and rubber are also found though it is less in quantity.

[35] Asoso Yonuo, *The Rising Nagas: A Historical and Political Study* (Delhi: Vivek Publishing House, 1974), 19. Hereafter, Asoso, *The Rising Nagas*.... Animals like mithun, cows, buffaloes, pigs, goats and fowls for the purpose of consumption and trade.

[36] M. P. Namthiurei, *The Great Awakening* (Tamenglong: Golden Jubilee Publication, 1972), 8-9. Hereafter, Namthiurai, *The Great*....

from the salt springs. This salt is said to be highly medicinal. On the whole, they are economically self-sufficient in the sense of meeting their needs for survival.

1.4. Religious belief and practices

The Zeliangrong people are religious by nature. From the beginning they are said to have had a very strong concept that every act they perform should be acceptable in the sight of God.[37] Their religious worldview is eco-friendly and holistic in nature. Some of their beliefs and practices are discussed below:

1.4.1. Belief in a Supreme Being

The Zeliangrong religion, though initially polytheistic in nature, had a strong monotheistic element which is found in the worship of the Supreme God, *Tinggwang or Tingkao Ragwang.* They believed in the existence of one supreme Deity called *Tinggwang,* King of Heaven or *Raguang,* King of the gods or Universal God.[38] He is also believed to have created the firmament and its bodies like the sun, moon and stars. He is invisible but all pervading. He is a good god. They took him to be neutral, and sacrifices were rarely offered to him because he gave no trouble to humankind. This *Tinggwang* or *Raguang* was worshipped so that their souls might go to another world and live.[39] The Zeliangrong also believed in the existence of a female deity called *Tingrangpui* or *Mideteikemlungbepui* who causes the birth of beings.

1.4.2. Pantheon of gods and deities

Their religion could also be described as polytheistic, a belief in multiple gods. Alternatively, it could be identified as henotheism as there was belief in and worship of one Supreme God out of many gods.[40] There was a belief in the pantheon of gods who were entrusted

---

[37] K. C. Gaila, "Religion and Politics in the Zeliangrong Context," Souvenir: *The 4th Youth Conference RNBA* (Tamenglong: RNBA Youth Department, 2003), 30.

[38] G. Makuga, *Introduction to the Rongmei Nagas...*, 93.

[39] Ramkhun, *The Zeliangrong Nagas...*, 34.

[40] Prof. Gangmumei Kamei, "The Concept of the Zeliangrong Religion" *Souvenir Tingkao Ragwang Kalum Kai* (Chingmeirong, Imphal: Zeliangrong Ra Chap-Riak Phom, 2001), 1-2.

with the affairs of humans, animals and things on earth. These gods were below the supreme God.

1.4.3. Belief in spirits

They also believed in the existence of spirits both benevolent and malevolent. They were believed to have separate residences in distinct places and exercised their power within their limitations.[41] Several spirits are still recognized by some Zeliangrong people, such as *Meizipui* who distribute and look after the crops; generally a pure white fowl is offered to her. *Renamra* is the spirit who guards, protects and keeps the village; a red cock is offered to him as sacrifice.[42]

1.4.4. Ancestor worship

There is no ancestor worship among the Zeliangrong people, contrary to what has been claimed by ill-informed writers and observers. However, there has been a belief that the souls of the dead do not go away too far, but often come back and visit the home. Therefore, they offered rice, curry and rice beer to the soul.[43] The Zeliangrong people conducted a religious rite called *Rekak* at the beginning of every year, to send off the spirits of the dead.[44]

1.4.5. Life after death

The Zeliangrong people also strongly believed in the immortality of soul, that when a person died, his/her soul was believed to go and live in a land called *Taruairam* or *Heruiram* meaning the "land of the dead." It was also believed that the dead person will meet their

---

[41] Ramkhun, *The Zeliangrong Nagas…*, 34. The most influential spirits are the spirits of agriculture called lau-ra. They are offered sacrifices for their care and protection of the crops and to yield good harvest. There is also a spirit called Nsuang-ra who resides in the village, caring and defending the village, and sacrifices were offered to them also. They also offered sacrifices to the malevolent spirits in order to propitiate and appease them so that those spirits might not cause trouble and disturb humankind.

[42] Verrier Elwin, *The Nagas in the Nineteen Century* (London: Oxford University Press, 1969), 423.

[43] Ramkhun, *The Zeliangrong Nagas…*, 36.

[44] Heisuiding, *Benreu Paupai Renet …*, 8.

progenitor in that world. Therefore, they performed rituals for the dead and gave his/her belongings to the dead with the concept that the death of a person is only the end of the first part of life whereby s/he begins another part of life.[45] They believed that the condition of life after death will be determined by the kind of life they lived on earth. If one led a bad life on earth, one will inherit bad life in the second stage, but if one led a good life on earth, one will go in peace and happiness to *Taruairam.*[46]

1.4.6. *Genna*: Practices and significance

The word *Genna* is known in Zeliangrong dialect as *keniu,* meaning 'forbidden' or 'restriction'. Observing *genna* is a common practice among the Zeliangrong people, just like the other Nagas. It may mean rest from work due to unusual natural phenomenon like earthquake, a first hail storm, lunar eclipses, solar eclipses, natural death, and village festivals. It is a day of prayer to the Supreme Being, giving thanks for His protection from dangers and submitting to His care and safety from the eminent dangers ahead, thus it is a prayer for the welfare of the community. There are different kinds of *Gennas* with different levels of intensity.[47]

1.5. Values highly regarded in Zeliangrong Society

1.5.1. Community Orientation

The Zeliangrong people are community loving people; they have a very strong sense of community feeling. This community orientation has enabled them to survive together down the centuries against all odds. They do everything together in group for the welfare of the community, and in doing it the individual also gets back his/her due

---

[45] G. Makuga, *Introduction to the Rongmei...*, 95-96.

[46] Ramkhun, *The Zeliangrong Nagas...*, 36.

[47] Some *keniu* affects the whole village, clan, or a family. On *keniu* days, no guest is entertained in the house so as to avoid the diseases and evil spirits that might be coming with the outsiders. In some *keniu*days the village gate was shut and no travelers were allowed to enter the village.

reward from the community.[48] They eat, drink, sleep, sing, dance, play, hunt, fish, construct houses, and do all their arduous task of cultivation together. All the burdens, hardships, sorrows, happiness and joy are shared together in group. Doing things together or exchange of labors in a rotation basis is called *hegwet* in Zeliangrong. Thus, an individual has his/her being in association with the community.

1.5.2. Sense of equality

The Zeliangrong society practice equality for everyone. Everyone in the society is given equal importance and due respect, there is neither class nor sexual distinction. Everyone has got their own role to play for the community; no family is ever left alone to the mercy of the circumstances without being attended by the community.[49] The Zeliangrong society is patriarchal and patrilineal. It appears to practise gender bias, because of the sexual work division, but both the sexes have equal dignity. As a result, the Zeliangrong women enjoy considerable liberty in the society.

1.5.3. Respect for elders

Respect for elders and parents have been the mark of good citizenship in the Zeliangrong society. They highly regard the aged people for their life experience and the wisdom they possess. Sacrifices were also performed by respected elders in the society. The Zeliangrong people set apart certain portion of meats for the aged peoples from the animals butchered for feasts or procured from their games; for example, the heart, liver, kidneys and some special portion of flesh. No doubt the Zeliangrong respect and obey the elders but they are

---

[48] M. Horam, *North East India: A Profile* (New Delhi: Cosmo Publications, 1990), 185.

[49] *A Brief Historical Account of Nagaland* (Kohima: Naga Institute of Culture, 1970), 162. Both the rich and the poor were given equal privileges to live in the village, build their houses, cultivate the land and rear cattle in the community land in addition to keeping their own private possessions.

obeyed only in so far as they are in harmony with the needs of the community.[50]

1.5.4. *Heleikerau*

The term *Heleikerau,* is also called *Leirau* in short, and literally means, "Not willing to be subordinated or inferior to others in doing any humanitarian activities of life". This principle of tribal ethics, found in other parts of NEI, is known by the Mizos as *Tlawmngaihna*[51] and by the Aos as *Sobaliba.*[52] This principle enabled the Zeliangrong people to protect themselves from traumas in the face of emergencies and difficult times like sickness, death and poverty, as every person is helped and cared for. The welfare of the community takes precedence over all things. Thus, the tribals live in community, work with community, and die for the community's sake.[53] The Zeliangrongs' adage says, "*Leirau* is better than knowledge and wisdom, wealth and bravery."[54] Persons who practice *leirau* are called *Heleikeraume;* they practice this principle in all aspects of life but no reward is given to them except the appreciation of the people.

Conclusion

As seen from the above deliberation, the Zeliangrong people share a common origin having common ancestors, common affinity and common cultural heritage, armoured by common experiences. They have been religious in their own way giving due reverence and

---

[50] V. Epao, *From Naga Animism to Christianity* (New Delhi: Sanjivan Press, 1993), 38. If an aged man walked in to *hangsiuki* the best seat would be given to him and the others would listen to what he would say, for the sayings of the aged are considered to be precious for they have their fulfillment in life. The presence of elderly people is a consolation and a blessing for the community on all occasions.

[51] Thanzauva, *Theology...,* 120.

[52] A. Wati Longchar, "Interaction Between Gospel and culture among the Nagas" *Encounter Between Gospel and Culture,* ed. by A. Wati Longchar (Jorhat: TSC., ETC., 1999), 55.

[53] Yangkahao, "Sources for Developing Tribal Theology," An Exploration of Tribal Theology, ed., A. Wati Longchar (Jorhat: Tzüdikong Baptist Church for the Tribal study centre, 1997), 67.

[54] Heisuiding, *Benreu Paupai Renet...,* 30.

honour to the one whom they believed to be divine and deserved to get their worship and sacrifices. They are a community who believe in and value the communitarian life, guided by the principle of *leirau*, in which all members of the community, young and old, male and female, have their role to play for the welfare of the community. With this information we will now see the advent of Christianity to the Zeliangrong people and their response to the Christian message.

Chapter 2

THE ADVENT OF CHRISTIANITY TO THE ZELIANGRONG NAGAS

Introduction

This chapter highlights how the gospel was first introduced to the Zeliangrong people, about the first converts, the response of the people to the gospel message and the role of the Zeliangrong *Heraka* cult and the traditional religion which obstructed the spread of the gospel among the people. The growth of the Baptist churches, formation of the Zeliangrong Baptist Association and the division of the Association is discussed. The chapter also highlights the various other Christian denominations which have been established in the region.

The establishment of the British Government in the Naga Hills hastened the spread of Christianity among the Nagas by the American Baptist Foreign Mission (ABFM) in the mid-19th century. Rev. Dr. E. W. Clark, pioneer American Missionary, arrived at the Sibsagar Mission in 1871, and he deputed Godhula, an Assamese Christian to Dekahaimong to spread the gospel. In November 1872, Godhula brought nine Ao Nagas to Sibagar to be baptized by Rev.

Dr. Clark. On their return, the converts built a chapel in their village in December 1872, and in the same year Dr. Clark was reported to have baptized 24 persons and the church of Christ began to grow in the Ao area.[1]

In 1878, another missionary, Rev. C. D. King was sent to the Naga Hills and he established a mission station at Kohima. On March 29, 1883, Rev. and Mrs. C. D. King, with four Assamese Christians, organized themselves into the Kohima Baptist Church. It was on June 21, 1885 that the first Angami Naga convert was baptized and became a member of this church.[2]

2.1. Zeliangrong people and Christianity

The advent of Christianity to the Zeliangrong community can be traced back to the Kohima field which was established in the year 1880, pioneered by Rev. C. D. King.[3] This field covered the Angamis, the Zeliangrongs, the Kukis, the Chakesangs, the Maos-Paomeis and the Rengmas. Benreu village in the Northern Zeliangrong area was the first village to embrace Christianity among the Zeliangrong Nagas.

2.1.1. Outsider Scholarship

Puthuvail Thomas Philip dates the first conversion among the Zeliangrong people to Christianity in 1905, based on the Missionary's Annual Report of 1906. The Report states that three students of the Kohima Mission School were baptized on December 31, 1905. One of them was listed as Kacha Naga, a former name used for

---

[1] A. Bendangyabang Ao, *History of Christianity in Nagaland: A Source Material* (Kohima: Shalom Ministry, 1998), 51.

[2] "A Glimpse of Nagaland Churches" *Nagaland Celebrates Quasqui Centennial: From Darkness to Light* (Kohima: NBCC, 1997), 14, 15. Initially these missionaries attempted to evangelize the Shan tribes of Northern Burma and Southern China, but they met the Nagas of *Namsung* village and evangelized them. However after five years the mission board diverted its focus towards the plain of Assam and stationed the mission at Sibsagar.

[3] Milton S. Sangma, *History of American Baptist Mission in North East India (1836-1950) Vol. 1* (Delhi: Mittal Publications, 1987), 240.

the Zeliangrong.[4] Dr. F. S. Downs records that, "the first Christian converts were Keneise and Nsarangbe of Benreu village, and they had been evangelized by an Angami. There was a full time Angami evangelist working in the Zeliangrong area. Though the name was not mentioned, in 1927 it was reported that a high school graduate was working as an Evangelist."[5] However, their reports do not match with the local traditions. The local traditions are discussed below.

2.1.2. The first converts and initial growth of Christianity according to tradition

The first convert as recorded in the souvenir of the Benreu Baptist Church Diamond Jubileeof 1981 was Mr. Heizieluing, son of Mr. Heluikieswang.[6] According to the record of C. D. King, on July 28, 1885 he baptized four Nagas at Kohima, three persons were from Kohima village namely Lhousetsu, Lhouselie and Sieliezhu, but the name of the fourth person was not mentioned. However, some clues lead the people to believe that that person could be Mr. Heizieluing, because he was reported to be engaged in construction works in the Mission compound from the very initiation of the Kohima field. A more informative report is found from Miss. Narola Rivenburge (daughter of Rev. Revenburge) who has recorded in a journal, "Star of Naga Hills", that Mr. Heizieluing went to Impur (Ao centre) on foot, walking 100 miles, to be baptized by Rev. Rivenburge in 1897.[7] After a gap of eight years, two more men were reported to

---

[4] Puthuvail Thomas Philip, *The Growth of Baptist Churches in Nagaland,* 2nd ed., (Guwahati: Christian Literature Centre, 1983), 124. Hereafter, P. T. Philip, *The Growth of Baptist Churches...*

[5] F. S. Downs, *The Mighty Works of God; A Brief History of the Council of Baptist Churches in NEI: The Mission Period 1836-1950* (Guwahati: CLC, 1971), 146-47. Hereafter, Downs, *The Mighty Works...*

[6] *Benreu Baptist Church Diamond Jubilee Souvenir* (Benreu: BBCDJC, 1981), 4. Hereafter, *BBC Diamond...*

[7] Benreu Baptist Church Centenary Feb. 7-9, 1997 Souvenir (Benreu: BBCCC, 1997), 19-20. Hereafter, *BBC Centenary*....It also said that Heizieluing had a very intimate relationship with the early Christians especially with Sieliezhu. Even though they did not have a consanguine relation, they spent weeks together at Sieliezhu's house. Therefore, it is believed that they were tied together for some special reasons such as the bonds of Christian love.

be baptized; these two could be Iriedaung and Heirielung,[8] and in 1914, Mr. Heizieluing's father and Mrs. Ileuteile, mother of Mr. Namkuheing were baptized at Kohima by Rev. Rivenburge during the third Kohima Zone Christian Association.[9] It is believed that the gospel penetrated to the second village Tampung in 1899. However, there was a halt 'till 1924. From 1925, people from more villages began to embrace the gospel.[10]

The gospel was first brought to the Liangmai area of Nagaland in 1926 by a Kuki evangelist, Rev. Ngulpu. The first Liangmai to embrace the gospel was Mr. Wisung from *Tening (Henima)* village. He took baptism in the year 1927 from Rev. Ngulpu.[11] Through his preaching Mr. Adinbou and other friends from *Ntuma* village heard the gospel and accepted the Lord and became Christians in 1933. Thus, the Christian faith began to increase among the Liangmais. On hearing the reports, Rev. Tanquist, the American Baptist Missionary of Kohima field, regularly visited and nurtured the new fellowship church.[12]

The Rongmei Nagas were in Nagaland since the British regime, particularly in Kohima and Dimapur. They settled there prior to the 1930s. They also established a village known as 'Ragailong Village'

---

[8] *BBC Diamond...*, 9.

[9] Ramkhun, *The Zeliangrong Nagas...*, 53.

[10] Mr. Suitei, Executive Secretary, "Zeme Baptist Church Council (ZBCC)" *From Darkness to Light: A Publication of the NBCC on the Occasion of the Celebration of 125 years of Christianity in Nagaland.* Kohima: NBCC, 1997. 90.

[11] Mr. Ramriwang, Executive Secretary, "Liangmai Baptist Association (LBA)" From Darkness to Light: A Publication of the NBCC on the Occasion of the Celebration of 125 years of Christianity in Nagaland. (Kohima: NBCC, 1997), 75-76. It is interesting to note that Wisong was born partially blind, but God chose him and used him mightily as an effective instrument for spreading the Christian faith among the Liangmai community. He could neither read nor write but he had a sharp memory power. He went to Kohima and learnt some scripture verses and some simple hymns in Angami, which he put to good use during his evangelical tours.

[12] Ramkhun, *The Zeliangrong Nagas...*, 57. There is a small sub-tribe of the Zeliangrongs known as "Puimei" which was known as "Kaupui" during the British period and thus even at present the Rongmeis are mistakenly called as "Kabui" derived from "Kaupui".

at Fullerganj Bazar area (the present New Market area) of Dimapur.[13] Rongmeis were called and known as "Kabuis" by the outsiders, which was a mistaken name.[14] The Rongmeis ardently believed and staunchly followed the traditional and customary practices of their forefathers.

However in the late sixties, Late Pantiful Kamei of Ragailong Village (Dimapur) accepted Jesus Christ as his personal Saviour in 1969. He was actively involved in evangelizing his people in the early 1970s.[15] In addition to this, the Revival awakening of the 1970s captured the hardened hearts of the Rongmeis to accept the gospel and embrace Christianity. Thus, the first Rongmei Baptist Church (RBC) was established at *Ragailong* Village Burma Camp, Dimapur in the year 1978.[16]

2.1.3. The opposition from the *Kampai* Cult or the *Heraka* religion

The church also faced a great persecution when the tribal cult called "Heraka" was revived. This movement was led by a seer called Jadonang, who had been a soldier in the First World War. On his return he prophesied the coming of a Naga Raj and the advent of prosperity for 'all who eat from the wooden platter' that is, all Nagas.[17] His aim was to unite the three kindred tribes of Nagas, the Zeme, Liangmai and Rongmei (Zeliangrong) to drive away the British and the Kukis who were considered as foreigners.[18] The objective of the uprising was a "socio religious reformation and political goal to separate the

---

[13] *Rongmei Baptist church Burma Camp, Silver Jubilee 1978-2003 Souvenir* (Dimapur: RBCBC, 2003), 1. Hereafter, RBC, *Silver ...*

[14] Ramkhun, *The Zeliangrong Nagas...*, 58.

[15] RBC, *Silver...*, 1, 2. Some devoted Christians like Mr. Wizibou, Rev. Hazieding, Rev. H. K. Lungalang and Mr. Lujim Thangkhul evangelized the Rongmei people. It is reported that Pantiful Kamei accepted the Lord while he was undergoing medical treatment at T. B. Leikol Hospital at Chingmeirong, Imphal.

[16] See Ramkhun, *The Zeliangrong Nagas...*, 58; RBC, *Silver...*, 3-4.

[17] Yonuo, *Rising Nagas...*, (Delhi: 1974), 126.

[18] K. S. Singh, ed., *Tribal Movement in India, Vol. I,* (New Delhi: Manohar Publications, 1982), 54. Hereafter cited as Singh, *Tribal Movement...*

Zeliangrong from the British regime and to establish a Naga Raj".[19] The means employed by the Zeliangrong Movement were essentially ritualistic. They also foretold the future and cured the sick in the traditional way, depending on shamans.[20] After a period of violent rebellion, before Jadonang could achieve his goal, he was implicated in a murder case, arrested and executed on 29th August, 1931. After his execution Gaidinliu, a seventeen year old lady led the movement by taking up armed forces but was later suppressed in 1932.[21]

Jadonang's religious ideals were crystallized in the *Heraka* cult by Gaidinliu who was regarded as his spiritual successor. The term *Heraka* is derived from the words *Hera* meaning "god" *and Kanchi* meaning "pure", and so the term *Heraka* connotes pure religion. Those who ridiculed this movement called it *Kampai* meaning "unsuccessful".[22] The *Heraka* cult which was revived by Gaidinliu spread over a large area of Naga Hills, Manipur and the North Cachar Hills of Assam. Later Gaidinliu was also arrested in September 1932 on the charge of murder and was sentenced to life imprisonment.[23] However, she was released by the Government in 1948 when India obtained independence from British rule. Following her release, the movement was revived. They adopted an anti-Christian stance.[24] They preached that the millennium was at hand; her influence upon

---

[19] Singh, *Tribal Movement…*, 56.

[20] Julian Jacobs, *The Nagas: Hill Peoples of Northeast India* (London: Thames and Hudson Ltd, 1990), 161. Hereafter, Julian, *The Nagas….* They established a new set of religious practices, including the setting up of purifying baths, shrines and clay statues of the gods of the reformed religion. Jadonang and Gaidinliu soon became the recipients of gifts of sacrificial cattle.

[21] Aosenba, *The Naga Resistance Movement: Prospect of Peace and Armed Conflict* (New Delhi: Regency Publications, 2001), 25. Hereafter, Aosenba, *The Naga Resistance …*

[22] Rajen Gonmei, "A Study of the Heraka Movement on the Socio, Political land Religious life of the Zeliangrong" (B. D. Thesis, Eastern Theological College, 1994), 43.

[23] Aosenba, *The Naga Resistance…*, 25, citing Sir Robert Reid, *History of the Frontier Areas Bordering Assam from 1883-1941*, (Eastern Publication House, 1983), 170-71.

[24] Ramkhun, *The Zeliangrong Nagas…*, 51-52.

the people was great until recently, when the movement began to decline.

The Zeliangrong people opposed the British administration and Christianity and looked to a different tradition, Hinduism, and remained less favorably disposed to the British. The *Heraka* movement had an irregular armed force and engaged themselves in violent clashes with the Federal Nagas, whom they regarded as too Christian and too anti-India, and remained on reasonably good terms with the Indian Government. The Zeliangrong Nationalist Movement seems to have accepted the legitimacy of the Indian constitution, though they argue for a united Zeliangrong Homeland. This is an unfulfilled dream of the people as they have been geographically trifurcated to three states of Northeast India (viz., Assam, Manipur and Nagaland).[25] The fight for a Zeliangrong Homeland was pacified by the award of Padmabushan to Rani Gaidinliu and by entering Jadonang's name in the list of the Indian freedom fighters.[26] However, the Zeliangrong *Heraka* today deserves a good deal of appreciation for preserving many good traditional songs and dances, attires and ornaments and retaining the past heritage of the Zeliangrong people.

2.2. Formation of Zeliangrong Baptist Association

Prior to 1926, the Zeliangrong churches were under the Kohima Mission field as they were few in number and too weak to stand alone. But when the Kohima Mission Field held its Annual Association at Chalkot from March 20-22, 1926, the joint Association of Zeliang and Kuki Christians was inaugurated and was called Zeliang-Kuki Baptist Association. According to the missionary report of 1937, the number of Zeliang-Kuki Christians was only 334.[27] The first pastors and evangelists were all paid by the Kohima Mission Field.[28] In 1939,

[25] Julian, *The Nagas...*, 163.

[26] Aninge H. Meriam, ed., *Zeliangrong Heraka Association Assam Nagaland Manipur: Silver Jubilee Closing Ceremony Souvenir* (Tening: 2000, Zeliangrong Heraka Association), 46.

[27] Milton S. Sangma, *History of ABM, Vol. 1...*, 264.

[28] Mr. Singsong, Executive Secretary, "Kuki Baptist Association (KBA)" *From Darkness to Light: A Publication of the NBCC on the Occasion o9f the Celebration*

Mr. Keneisie of Benreu Baptist Church was ordained by Rev. J. E. Tanquist and appointed to work as an evangelist for their areas.[29] In those days, the Angami dialect was used, and as a result all their resolutions were written in Angami. In 1951, H. K. Lungalang became the first Field Director of the Zeliang-Kuki Association. In 1953, the Kukis separated and formed their own association on the ground of the "dialect problem" and ended the Zeliang-Kuki Association. Eventually in January 1954, the Zeliang Baptist Association (ZBA) was organized from Ntu Baptist Church, instituting its centre at Ndunglwa village.[30] But, due to Naga political problems in those days, for security reasons the center was shifted to Peren Town, the then political headquarters of the tribe. Subsequently, the ZBA was affiliated to the Nagaland Baptist Church Council (NBCC). Soon after that, H. K. Lungalang was ordained by Rev. Dileno at Mission Center, Peren, and appointed as full time Field Director. There were also traveling pastors who traveled from village to village helping the churches. As a result, eight new churches were planted soon. By the end of 1955, there were 21 churches with 637 baptized Christians.[31]

During the early 1960s, when "The Zeliangrong Home Town" was established at Kabeikamning all the Zeliangrong people began to live together, and the Churches and Christian population rapidly increased in this area. Therefore, to accommodate everyone, the name of the Association was changed to "Zeliangrong Baptist Association" (Nagaland) in 1966.[32] In the year 1981, the Association in its Annual

---

of 125 years of Christianity in Nagaland. (Kohima: NBCC, 1997), 74. Hereafter, Singsong, *From Darkness...* The early pastors were Mr. Ngulpu and Mr. Keniese Zeliang and the evangelists were Mr. Sojang and Mr. Houbing.

[29] *BBC Diamond...*, 12.

[30] *BBC Centenary...*, 31.

[31] P. T. Philip, *The Growth of Baptist Churches...*, 125.

[32] See *BBC Centenary...*, 46; see Ramkhun, *The Zeliangrong Nagas...*, 55. During the Naga independence movement throughout the Naga inhabited areas by the Naga National Council (NNC), the Zeliangrong People from Assam Manipur and Nagaland joined the NNC and formed one Army contingency. They travelled across their land in their underground set and discovered the unexploited Kabeikamning present Jalukie valley which were owned by the peoples of Jalukie, Mhai, and Samziuram. The fertile land was not exploited for habitation due to the presence of wild animals, it seemed dangerous to human life and at the same time

Council resolved to change its nomenclature to Zeliangrong Baptist Church Council ZBCC (N), and this resolution was implemented from 1982 after the Annual Council at Mpung village.[33]

2.3. Division of the Zeliangrong Baptist Church Council

The churches continued to grow under the banner of Zeliangrong Baptist Church Council, Peren Centre. However, as the church began to grow towards maturity, the people felt the need to form their own separate Associations. As Donald McGavran, the pioneer in church growth study has pointed out, the basis for church growth is to concentrate first on the same linguistic group for the fast and firmer growth of the church.[34] This saying was true in the context of the Zeliangrong Church, as the Zeliangrong people do not have a common language but speak four slightly different dialects, thus they began to form their own separate churches for their convenience and for the effective growth of the church.

2.3.1. Liangmai Baptist Aruang LBA (Tening Town)

The Liangmai Baptist Association, Aruang Centre is at Tening which has also been the government centre since the British days. As the churches began to grow, the Liangmai group felt the need to form

---

the climate was too hot for habitation as well as cultivation. The Zeliangrong people unanimously decided to settle there to establish "The Zeliangrong Home Town" in this valley, and established themselves during the early 1960s. Rev. Bikau Pame worked as the second Field Director of this Association from 1976-1984. During his time, the membership was reported to be 6000 baptized members with 62 churches and the total Christian population was 24,280.

[33] See Suitei, comp., *Zeme Baptist Church Council (N): Pe reha, petah nah pe macet-mariam* (Peren Town: Published by the Compiler, 2002), 30. Hereafter, Suitei, *ZBCC...*: *BBC Centenary...*, 46. Rev. H. Visor was the third Executive Secretary of the Association (1984 – June, 1987). By this time the title Field Director was changed to Executive secretary, After Rev. Visor left the Association for a higher calling to serve the Council of Naga Baptist Churches as the General Secretary in 1987, Rev. H. K. Lungalang worked again as the fourth Executive Secretary for a year July 1987-Feb. '88, the fifth was Rev. Ramyi Hau 1988-1993, the sixth was Rev. Suitei from 1993-2003 and the seventh ES. is Rev. Kuzierang Thou from 2004 – till date.

[34] Ramkhun, *The Zeliangrong Nagas...*, 59.

their own separate Association for their convenience. Therefore, the Liangmai churches requested the approval of ZBCC to have a Liangmai Churches Fellowship (N) in 1981. The issue was discussed in the following two ZBCC Councils, in 1982 at Peren Town Baptist Church and in 1983 at Peren.When the leaders of the Council met in January 27, 1984 at Kejanglwa village,[35] the house finally resolved for the formation of a separate Liangmai Baptist Association, with Mr. Ramriwang as their Executive Secretary.[36] At present this association has 18 local churches and 3 fellowships with about 5000 baptized members. LBA has 11 office staff, 4 ordained ministers and 4 licentiates. Rev. Kitanwi Chewang is the present Executive Secretary.[37]

2.3.2. Zeme Baptist Association-Nsong (ZBA-N)

Mr. Hairangaung of Nsong Village was the first convert among the Southern Zeme group; he became a Christian in the year 1954. In the year 1972, the Southern Zeme Christian brethren formed a "Pastors and Deacons Fellowship" at Lalong Baptist church, and in 1977 the fellowship changed its name to Zeme Baptist Fellowship, Nagaland. In 1985 the fellowship requested the ZBCC executive committee to form their own association, but the committee did not recommend it and even the 1986 ZBCC council at Heningkunglwa referred the matter to the next executive committee for better consideration. However, the Zeme Baptist Fellowship met at Nsong Baptist Church in March 1986 and organized themselves into the Zeme Baptist Association (ZBA) Nagaland stationed at Nsong, with Mr. Deisam Pame (1986-1999) as Executive Secretary. ZBA got its recognition from the Nagaland Baptist Church Council in 1997. The main reasons for forming a separate association were dialectical inconveniences, and transport and communication problems over

---

[35] Suitei, *ZBCC…*, 56.

[36] Ramkhun, The Zeliangrong Nagas…, 58. See Elungkiebe Zeliang, *Charismatic Movements in the Baptist Churches in North East India: A Zeliangrong Perspective* (Delhi: ISPCK, 2014), 46. Hereafter Zeliang, *Charismatic Movement…*

[37] Rev. Kitanwi, ES, LBA, telephone interview, 4 April 2018. See Rev. Kamwang Rentta, LBA Executive Secretary Report at NBCC 71st Annual Session at Kiusor, February, 1-3, 2008. Hereafter Kamwang, ES Report…

the vast geographical area.[38] It has 13 local churches with around 1500 baptized members, and Mr. Ariebo is the Executive Secretary of the Association at present.[39]

2.3.3. Rongmei Baptist Association (RBA) Jalukie Town

The RBA was formed on May 5, 1988 at Ragailong, Burma Camp, Dimapur. The reason for its formation was the effect of the decision taken on 'Nomenclature policy' by the ZBCC in its Annual Session at Poilwa on 29th January 1988. It was also for the purpose of maintaining one's own literature among Zeliangrong people. Hence the RBA was established on the aforementioned day with its Centre at Jalukie Town.[40] Mr. Meijaolung was appointed as the first Executive Secretary.[41] Currently RBA has 8 local churches, 5 fellowships, 3500 baptized members, 11 missionaries sent to Arunachal and Assam. Mr. Mathiuthai is the present Executive Secretary.[42]

2.3.4. Zeme Baptist Church Council (ZBCC) Peren

With the departure of the Liangmai churches in 1984 and the Southern Zeme churches in 1986, the Zeliangrong Baptist church Council was left with only the Rongmei and the Northern Zeme group. Therefore, the Council considered its nomenclature in its Annual Session at Poilwa on 29th January 1988, and decided to use the name Zeme Baptist Church Council (N).[43] The new nomenclature has excluded the Rongmei people who are still remaining in the ZBCC (N), as a result, the Rongmei group also formed the RBA Nagaland centered at Jalukie Town in the year 1988. Since then, the Zeme group has been continuing to use the nomenclature Zeme Baptist Church Council ZBCC (N). Currently ZBCC (P) has 67 local churches with 18,093 baptized members, 10 ordained ministers,

---

[38] Interview with D. Kupwa Zeme, Acting Pastor, Zeme Baptist Church, Peren Town, 19th October, 2008. Hereafter, Interview, *D. Kupwa…*

[39] Teubei, Former ES, ZBA, telephone interview, 3rd April 2018.

[40] *20th Foundation Day of Rongmei Baptist Association Nagaland,* May 5, 2008. Hereafter, *20th Foundation RBA….*

[41] Ramkhun, *The Zeliangrong Nagas…,* 59.

[42] Mathiuthai, Executive Secretary, RBA, telephone interview, 5 April 2018.

[43] Suitei, *ZBCC…,* 30.

14 licentiates, 4 evangelists, 3 project heads (ZBCC Prayer center, BHSS Peren and BHS Jalukie) and 11 office sitting staff members. Mr. Izieteilung is the present Executive Secretary of this council.[44]

2.3.5. Zeme Baptist Association-Jalukie (ZBA-J)

The Zeme Baptist Association-Jalukie (ZBA-J) headquartered at Jalukie Town is the youngest association of the Zeliangrong Baptist Church Associations (ZBCAs). Before the formation of ZBA-J, there were three Zeme Baptist Associations, viz., Zeme Naga Baptist Association (ZNBA) Manipur, Zeme Baptist Association-Asalu (ZBA-A) Assam and Zeme Baptist Association-Nsong (ZBA-N) Nagaland, and the triad was working together in an organization called Zeme Baptist Union (ZBU) for about 30 years. Then they desired to have an amalgamated body of all the three Zeme Baptist Associations to one body. Thus, they had numbers of consultations and finally on 2011 they inaugurated the Zeme Baptist Association (ZBA) at Jalukie Town. They also made a declaration to surrender all properties to the Centre and to make the previous three Association Centres to a sub-center under ZBA-J. However, they are not free from all problems in their unification, because the newly amalgamated association was denied for their affiliation to Nagaland Baptist Church Council (NBCC), because the jurisdiction of the former covers Assam, Manipur and Nagaland while the latter confines to Nagaland alone, so the ZBA-J is affiliated to the Fellowship of Naga Baptists Associations (FNBA) headquartered at Dimapur, Nagaland. When the affiliation to NBCC failed, some few churches previously under ZBA-Nsong Nagaland withdrew themselves from ZBA-J and opted to remain as ZBA-Nsong.[45]

Currently ZBA-J has 69 local churches with little more than 6000 members, 12 ordained ministers and around 40 missionaries.

---

[44] Mr. Izieteilung, Executive Secretary, ZBCC Peren, telephone interview, 9 April 2018. Hereafter, Izieteilung, telephone interview….

[45] Dr. Rabi Pame, Chairman Ordination Committee ZBA-J, telephone interview, 4 April 2018.

The association has 11 office sitting staff and Rev. Sahingmak is the present Executive secretary.[46]

2.4. Other Denominational Church Traditions

As the church continued to grow in the region, the people also developed contacts with various denominational Christian groups which were also extending their mission. As a result, quite a few Zeliangrong people also converted to various denominations. There is little available information regarding these smaller groups, but a brief overview of each is presented here.

2.4.1. Roman Catholic

The Roman Catholic mission reached Kohima in 1948 and established its mission in the succeeding years. It reached the Zeliangrong people in Peren district in the last part of 1964 in the person of Fr. Felix. He came from Kohima and started the Catholic mission[47] by opening All Saints Home Cambridge School, Peren in March 1965. Thus, the seed of the Catholic faith took root among the Zeliangrong people in Peren district. They run educational institutions in the three main towns of Peren district, viz., Peren, Jalukie and Tening. Today a good number of people in Peren district are educated from Catholic-run institutions, and as a result, seven Catholic churches are established in Peren District.[48]

2.4.2. Christian Revival

The Nagaland Christian Revival Church (NCRC) is another significant denomination. Kohima is the centre of NCRC for all of Nagaland. The Angami Christian Revival mission extended to the Zeliangrong people in Peren District. There are eleven Christian

---

[46] Rev. Sahingmak, Executive Secretary ZBA-J, telephone interview, 5 April 2018.

[47] Angeline Lotsüro, *The Nagas: A Missionary Challenge* (Shillong: Vendrame Institute Publications, 2000), 60. Hereafter Angeline, *The Nagas…* It is said that Mr. Namgangheing, the then chairman of the Zeliangrong Tribal Council, invited Catholic missionaries to come and open Catholic schools in the area.

[48] Zeliang, *Charismatic Movements…*38.

Revival Churches in Peren District.[49] *Ncangram* village is reported to be the first to embrace this denomination in 1983 and is also considered to be the center of Christian Revival Churches in Peren District.[50]

2.4.3. Presbyterian

There are also a good number of Zeliangrong people in Peren district who are members of the Presbyterian denomination. This denomination came to the Zeliangrong people in Peren District from their contact with their brethren living in the North Cachar Hills of Assam (recently called as Dima Hasao district), as many of them are from Presbyterian tradition. The Welsh Prebyterian mission reached the Zemes in Assam and made their first convert in 1910 by converting Mr. Dituing of Malangpeuram. In 1956, the first Zeme Presbytery was established and headquartered at Lodiram, and the Nreibak Presbytery was created in 1994, headquartered at Longmang. At present the Zeme Presbytery has six districts including Kabaikam district with six churches and Jalukie district with five churches.[51] These local churches are found in Jalukie Town, Samziuram, Beisumpuikam, New Beisumpuikam, Nsenlo, Nkio kam, Ngam, New Ngaulong, Khelma, Beisumpuilo and in Beisumpui villages of Peren district.[52]

2.4.4. Seventh Day Adventist

There are seven churches of the Seventh Day Adventists in Peren District.[53] Samziuram is the first village to have this denomination. There are around 500 baptized members from Zeliangrong

---

[49] Punglwa A, B, Gaili, Ngwalwa, Jalukie Town, Jalukie Jangdi, Samziuram, Peren Town, Ncangram, Tening and Tepun.

[50] Interview with Vechilhu, Prayer Chairman, Christian Revival Prayer House Jalukie, 18 October 2008. Ref. also to Zeliang, *Charismatic Movement*...39.

[51] Zeliang, *Charismatic Movement*...37. Mbeu district with eight churches is in Manipur and the other districts are in Assam.

[52] Interview with Stephen, Chairman, Presbyterian Church of North East India, Samziuram, 18 October 2008.

[53] Nzao, Peren Town, Samziuram (2 Churches), New Jalukie, Jalukie Town and Mhainamtsi.

community. The churches in Peren District are under Walford Dimapur, Headquarters of the Seventh Day Adventist church in Nagaland. Gonthan is the Pastor of Peren and Zunheboto districts.[54]

2.4.5. Pentecostal

The Pentecostal mission came to Kohima in 1961, and the first Zeliangrong to embrace this denomination was Mr. T. Zeliang from Poilwa village followed by others. The first Pentecostal church in Zeliangrong area was established in 1982 at Poilwa Namci, followed by establishing of churches in Poilwa, Ngwalwa and Jalukie town. Their branch office is in Dimapur, Nagaland. Their main Headquarters is in Chennai.[55] As their tradition practices sister/brotherhood they were reported to have more than five sisters among the Zeliangrong Pentecostals.[56]

2.4.6. Independent church

There is also another denomination known as the Independent church among the Zeliangrong community who are also sometimes called the Christian Baptist Church. The churches of this denomination are found in Ntu, Samziuram and Lungwiram villages.[57] During the 1977 revival movement the Ntu Baptist Church was divided because leadership did not like it, so the members who approved the revival movement formed a new church called Ntu Baptist Church and joined the ZBCC. The group that does not approve the revival movement remained in the Old Ntu Baptist church and detached themselves from the ZBCC; they remained an independent church.[58]

---

[54] Interview with Heigumchube, a member of Seventh Day Adventist Church, Peren Town, 19 October 2008.

[55] Interview with Brother in charge of Jalukie Town Pentecostal Church, 18 October 2008. See Zeliang, *Chrismatic Movement...*, 38.

[56] Brothers and sisters are those who committed themselves to serve the Lord and the church as full time workers.

57 Interview with Kerugai, Pastor Samziuram Baptist Church, 18 October 2008. Hereafter, interview with Kerugai..., Lungwiramis under Dimapur District but they are in close association with the two churches in Peren District.

[58] Zeliang, *Charismatic Movement...*, 39.

Conclusion

In the above discussion we have seen the coming of Christianity among the Zeliangrong people. At the first phase, Christianity appeared to be uniting the Zeliangrong people as one people under one ecclesiastical organization known as the Zeliangrong Baptist Association. However, within a short time of its existence the church was divided into various associations, thus the strength of the Association has been weakened and the unity of the people hindered. Could this be due to the tribal ethos? Is it because of the influence of the gospel or because of the misappropriation of both? These questions are left unanswered. Therefore, in the following chapter we will be looking into the encounter between the gospel and the Zeliangrong traditional life. Through such a study we hope to discover the influence of the traditional culture on Zeliangrong Christianity. It will enable us to understand the nature of the identity of Zeliangrong Christian and the problems related to their identity.

Chapter 3

THE ENCOUNTER/INTERACTION BETWEEN THE ZELIANGRONG CULTURE AND CHRISTIANITY

Introduction

As the gospel spreads over the world, it encounters various barriers. Human culture, religions, and social and political institutions becomes obstacles for the progress of the gospel. Christianity has struck its root deep among the tribals and brought far reaching changes in many spheres of tribal life and thought in the North East India.[1] The encounter between the two has brought many new developments, however in this chapter we shall deal only with the influence of the traditional and cultural practices upon the Zeliangrong Christians.

[1] S. K. Barpujari "Christianity and its Impact on the Nagas" ed., S. Karotemprel, 106-107. The gospel preached by the missionaries did away with many evil practices. Constant warring against one another and the spirit of hostility was replaced by love. Though valuable services were rendered to tribals in terms of education, social change and developments, yet the missionaries condemned the tribals' food, festivals, dress, ornaments, religious beliefs, communal institutions and mode of living. Tribals were discouraged to perform sacrifices with appropriate invocations of the spirits, Christian hymns and western songs replaced the traditional music and dances which were used extensively in the past. There was discontinuance of *Hangsiuki* (boys' dormitories) and community feasts by the tribal Christians at large.

Firstly, for better understanding of the issue, culture is first defined and the relation of culture to gospel is discussed. Secondly, the encounter and the result of the encounter, that is, the influence of the Zeliangrong culture on the Christians is studied under two periods of the Zeliangrong Church history, viz., from 1897-1953 when the Zeliangrong Churches were depending on the Kohima Mission Field and from 1954 till present when the church became free from dependence on others. Finally, the continuity of Zeliangrong culture in the life of the Zeliangrong Christians is traced, and drawn to a conclusion.

3.1. Culture defined

There are several definitions of culture. However, we shall be content with a general understanding of the term. According to Kraft, 'Culture is not in and of itself either an enemy or a friend to God or humans.' He further said that God as creator must be interested in human culture. 'God created humanity with at least the capacity for culture.'[2] We understand culture as "that complex whole which includes knowledge, belief, art, law, morals, customs, and any other capabilities and habits acquired by man as a member of society."[3] Culture is a way of life or the total plan for living, which is functionally organized into a system, and which is acquired through learning. It is the way of life of a social group, not of an individual as such.[4] Thus, to put it in the simplest terms, culture is a distinctive way of life embracing the total human-made response to the environment of a particular society of people. It is human beings' way of organizing themselves for living together.

---

[2] Roger E. Hedlund, *God and the Nations; A Biblical Theology of Mission in the Asian Context* (Delhi: ISPCK, 1997), 269. Hereafter, Roger, *God and the Nations...*

[3] E. Tylor, *Primitive Culture, Researches into the Development of Mythology, Philosophy, Religion, Art and Custom* (London, 1871), 1.

[4] L. J. Luzbetak, *The Church and Culture. New Perspectives in Missiological Anthropology* (Maryknoll: Orbis Books, 1988), 60.

3.2. Relation of Gospel and culture

Culture plays an important role in evangelization and mission takes place in the context of a people's culture and religion. Mission must be considered against the background of the non-biblical faiths and the cultures of the people represented.[5] In mission it is important to recognize the values found in any civilization and culture. God is not against culture, but he is against its perversions and expression of depravity. Human culture reflects aspects of both the Creator and the demonic realm.[6]

The matter of culture affects every aspect of mission. It is all-pervasive. If we ignore the influence of culture we run the risk of seriously misreading situations. It is true that the gospel is genuinely trans-cultural. However, it can only be expressed in terms of culture, and therefore, has to be reordered from one culture to another in a rich variety of ways.[7] The gospel is for all, and to understand this gospel, people have to hear from their own language (Acts 2:8). The message, though having a divine origin, is conveyed through human channels (2 Cor. 4:7). Therefore, we shall now look into the encounter of the gospel with the Zeliangrong culture and see the influence of culture in the life of the Zeliangrong Christians.

3.3. Encounter between the Zeliangrong Culture and Christianity (1897-1953) – Phase 1

The Zeliangrong traditional culture did not produce a favorable climate in most of the Zeliangrong communities for their first encounter with the gospel. The gospel or Christianity as a religion was seen as a foreign religion by the Zeliangrong people, because the kind of message that they preached and the lifestyle that they followed was not similar to that of the Zeliangrong traditional life. The Christian missionaries too had committed the mistake of looking at the traditional life style as uncivilized, demonic and dirty. The

[5] Roger, *God and the Nations...*, 132.

[6] Roger, *God and the Nations...*, 133.

[7] J. Andrew Kirk, *What is Mission? Theological Explorations* (London: Darton, Longman and Todd Ltd, 1999), 75. Hereafter, Kirk, *What is Mission?...*

traditional practices were considered as having no importance for Christian lives, thus they preached against the traditional practices.

The traditional Zeliangrong people also strongly resisted the spread of the gospel and the growth of churches in their society, seeing the spread of gospel and Christianity as a threat to their tradition and life. It was not only the Zeliangrong traditionalists but also the new cult called *Heraka,* (the reformists of the traditional religion which had sprung up during 1930s) which gave much hindrance for the spread of the gospel in the region. The nature of the encounter and influences will be discussed below.

3.3.1. The Zeliangrong Christians within the Kohima Mission Field 1897-1953

During the period when the Zeliangrong churches were under the Kohima Mission Field, the Zeliang-Kuki Association was formed in 1926. However, they were supervised by the missionaries at Kohima field, and they were reported to be still depending on the Kohima Mission Field in terms of monetary help and also ministerial works.[8] The foreign missionaries in those days (19th and early 20th centuries) generally assumed that churches "on the mission field" would be modeled on churches "at home." The tendency was to reproduce almost exact replicas.[9]

---

[8] See *Zeliangrong Baptist Association Nagaland Silver Jubilee 1954-1979,* (Peren: ZBAN Silver Jubilee Souvenir Committee, 1979), 11. Hereafter, Souvenir, *ZBAN…*, see Mr. Singsong, *From Darkness to Light…*, 74.

[9] The Lausanne Committee for World Evangelization, "The Willowbank Report" Perspectives: On the World Christian Movement, Third edt., eds., Ralph D. Winter & Steven C. Hawthorne (Pasadena: William Carey Library, 1999), 497, 498. Hereafter, Willowbank Report… The claim was that gothic architecture, prayer book liturgies, clerical dress, musical instruments, hymns and tunes, decision-making processes, synods and committees, superintendents and archdeacons-all were exported and unimaginatively introduced into the new mission founded churches. It should be added that these patterns were also eagerly adopted by the new Christians, determined not to be at any point behind their western friends, whose habits and ways of worship they had been attentively watching. But all this was based on the false assumptions that the Bible gave specific instructions about such matters and that the home churches' pattern of government, worship, ministry and life were themselves exemplary.

During this time, the influence of the outsiders was comparatively strong in the life of the Zeliangrong Christians. As the new converts were not properly guided, they were led to think that the cultural life and its practices were evil and un-Christian. In the words of H. Richard Niebuhr, such an approach could be described as '*Christ against Culture*,'[10] Christian life was considered to require a new and separated community, as something different and peculiar from cultural life and practices. As such, very little effort for indigenizing Christianity is seen in this period.

3.3.1.1. The missionaries' attitudes

The missionaries in the past had little or no positive attitude towards the Naga culture. Many writers agree that missionaries were not sympathetic to the cultures of the people and they blamed the missionaries as the main culprit for the disintegration of the culture. Takatemjen was right in agreeing with Christopher King who wrote that, in the Naga culture the missionaries intended to preserve very little and, looking for a faster pace of change, they were not interested in learning about the Nagas as Nagas.[11] They looked to Christ as the '*Transformer of Culture*.'[12] Accordingly they preached against the traditional lifestyle, food habits and social customs.

3.3.1.2. Missionaries' failures

No missionary had ever attempted to learn the dialect of the Zeliangrong people, but made them learn Angami dialect in order to know the word of God written in that dialect which was, in fact, a big hindrance for the people to have access to the word of God. They also sang hymns in Angami lyrics, with western tunes, as they thought that the Zeliangrong traditional tunes were inappropriate and associated with pride, romance and patriotism, and not in line

---

[10] H. Richard Niebuhr, *Christ and Culture* (New York: Harper & Row, Publishers, 1951), 48-49. Hereafter, Niebuhr, *Christ and Culture*.... Christ against culture implies that culture is the only authority and the claim of culture is to be rejected.

[11] Takatemjen, *Studies on Theology and Naga Culture* (Jorhat: CTC, Aolijen, Mokokchung, 1997), 13.

[12] Niebuhr, *Christ and Culture*... 193-196.

with the gospel. The missionaries did not help the people to praise God in their own traditional tunes but taught them the western hymns and western tunes. It was only in 1918, after 21 years of Christianity, that "Hymns in Kacha Naga," consisting of 12 hymns, was translated by Mr. Guizang, (the son of the first convert) which Rev. J. E. Tanquist arranged into a copy form.[13]

3.3.1.3. Failures of the native converts

In spite of their preaching against the traditional practices and cultural way of life, it is reported that the early missionaries allowed the local evangelists to drink locally brewed rice beer even in their evangelical tours.[14] According to Rev. Deuhing, it was not the missionaries who rejected and condemned the traditional practices and cultural life of the people, but it was the local Christians who felt guilty and considered it inappropriate to continue those practices. Therefore, they neglected it due to their obedience to the new faith, but without any deep understanding of these and other questions of culture and morality in the context of Christian life. However, we can also state that the missionaries had failed to give proper teaching and guidance to their new converts about these matters.

3.3.1.4. Problems and difficulty of the early converts

Indeed, conversion is not the automatic renunciation of all inherited culture. True conversion involves repentance, and repentance implies renunciation. Yet this does not require the convert to step right out of his/her former culture into a Christian sub-culture which is totally distinctive. It is imperative to learn how to distinguish between gospel and culture, and acknowledge those things in culture which are good and may therefore be retained, even transformed and enriched. However, the western churches demanded from every new member not only a conversion but also a change in culture.[15] Christians

---

[13] Suitei, *ZBCC…*, 86.

[14] Interview with Deuhing Nsa, an Ordain minister of the ZBCC, Peren Town, 10 January 2009. Hereafter, Interview with Deuhing….

[15] John R. W. Stott, *Christian Mission in the Modern World* (Bombay: Gospel Literature Service, 4th Reprint 1993), 122. Hereafter, John Stott, *Christian Mission….*

need great wisdom to discern between what may be retained and what must be renounced. But the Zeliangrong Christians adopted too negative an attitude to their former culture, leading to strong opposition from their own society. Even the Scripture has testified that when the Jews accused Stephen of teaching that, 'this Jesus of Nazareth will… change the customs which Moses delivered to us' and when some merchants of Philippi accused Paul and Silas of 'disturbing our city' because they advocated customs which were not lawful for 'Romans to accept or practice' (Acts 6:14 16:21, 22) the people strongly objected to such approaches. Culture consists of customs, and people feel threatened when their customs are disturbed.[16]

The missionaries failed to differentiate the gospel from culture and equated the gospel with their own mono-cultural background. This further led them to impose their own cultural lifestyle and customs on the converts. Consequently, the gospel has been seen as being foreign in general and western in particular. Thus, people rejected it, not because they rejected the Lordship of Christ but because conversion often meant a denial of their cultural heritage and social ties.[17]

3.3.1.5. Imposition of rules over the Christians by the non-Christians

When a person accepted Christ as his/her personal Savior and converted to the Christian faith, s/he was confronted with many hardships and difficulties, which were imposed by the non-Christians of the village. As the aforementioned Benreu village was the first among the Zeliangrong villages to embrace Christianity, in this village the non-Christians imposed restrictions upon the Christians. If the Christians could not abide by the restrictions of the non-

---

[16] John Stott, *Christian Mission…*, 123.

[17] Paul G. Hiebert, *Anthropological Insights for Missionaries* (Grand Rapids, Michigan: Baker Book House, 1998), 53. Hereafter, Hiebert, *Anthropological Insights ….*

Christians, they were to be moved out from their village and settle at a place some 3 miles away from their village.[18]

3.3.1.6. Casting out from the village community

Many other Zeliangrong villages cast out the Christians from their villages. For example, New Tesen was established in 1952 as life with the traditionalists was difficult for the Christians.[19] As a result, family ties were broken and some even lost their right of inheritance for embracing the new faith. Human beings are social creatures and dependent upon one another for survival and meaningful existence. They need care in childhood and old age. They find their greatest joy and fulfillment in the company of others. Social isolation is among the greatest punishments that could be inflicted upon humans,[20] and this was done to them by their fellow citizens for the sake of their new faith in Christ.

There were also yearly and seasonal *keniu* days and festivals of villages during these days no outsiders and strangers were permitted to enter the village. Once during his evangelistic tour, Mr. Sentonbe was persecuted by Peren villagers for violating their *keniu* by crossing their village.[21]

3.3.2. The resistance movement of Zeliangrong Heraka Cult

In addition to the opposition from their traditional religious people, the *Zeliangrong Heraka* Cult was another great resistance movement which restricted the spread of the gospel in the Zeliangrong region,

[18] Heisuiding, *Benreu Paupai Renet...*, 5.

[19] Interview with Hialung Kauring, a retired government servant, Peren Town, 19 November 2008. Similarly, interview with Ms. Chirailule, grand daughter of Mr. Songha (L), 19 November 2008 who reported that Late Songha the first convert from *Mbaupunggwa* village was chased out from the village, the villagers saying that even his corpse was not allowed to be buried in the village, thus he went out from the village and established a new Village called *Nkialwa.*

[20] Hiebert, *Anthropological Insights ...*, 51.

[21] Haisuitei, "A Historical study of Christianity and Heraka (kampai) cult among the Zeliangrong people of Nagaland" (B.D. thesis Bangalore, United Theological College, 1989). Hereafter, Haisuitei, *A Historical Study...*Evangelists of those days often slept outside the village gate without any contact with people. These *keniu* days are observed in most of the villages.

as they were explicitly and violently against Christianity.[22] There were sporadic persecutions of Christians in some villages, where they were not allowed to enter for preaching, and newly converted Christians were expelled from the village and their homes were further demolished.

Even during the 1950s and 1960s there was a revitalization and militarization of the *Heraka (Kampai)* cult movement, which affected the church life in one or the other way. The aggressive attitude of the movement towards the Christians hampered Christian mission. The church's annual report of this period repeatedly underlined the unfavourable situation created by the *Heraka* movement. The annual report of 1966 highlights the situation as;[23]

> For the last six or seven years the religious fanatics under Rani Gaidinliu are troubling us. They eat, drink, and dance and perform human sacrifices. They (are) opposed to Christianity. For the last few years it was not safe for anyone to travel in our area alone. In January last they killed eight persons.

Thus, it is clear that there was strong opposition from this group who tried to safeguard the traditions and the reformed religion of the Zeliangrong people. In fact, they could have preserved and retained the good culture and traditions without confronting the Christians, but unfortunately they had opposed Christianity and its growth massively in the past.

3.4. Encounter between the Zeliangrong Culture and Christianity (1953 – till date) – Phase 2

3.4.1. Zeliangrong Baptist Association

The Zeliangrong Baptists formed a separate Association, being independent from others, in 1953. They had their own authority to decide anything deemed fit for their churches and council. The three-self theory of Henry Venn and Rufus Anderson is strongly

---

[22] Downs, *The Mighty Works…*, 147.

[23] Council of Baptist Churches North East India Annual Reports, 1966, 74.

reflected in the life of the Zeliangrong churches in that period.[24] By the second half of the 20th century the need for indigenous leadership was realized and so they recruited or trained the local leaders. Yet, these local church leaders were indoctrinated in western ways of thought and procedure. These westernized local leaders preserved a very western-looking church, and the foreign orientation has persisted, only lightly cloaked by the appearance of indigeneity.[25] However, during this period there were numerable developments of indigenization in the life of the Zeliangrong churches as we shall see in the following discussion.

3.4.1.1. Translation of Scripture

The gospel of Matthew was translated by H. K. Lungalang in the year 1954, and the book was printed in 1957. The gospel of John was again translated and printed by Mr. Keneisie in 1961.[26] The rest of the books in the Bible were not yet translated. Therefore, they used the Angami Bible known as *Ketholeshü*.

3.4.1.2. Translation of Hymns

It was in the year 1956, that the Hymn book (1st edition) in Zeme dialect was produced by Khrietsovi Meru and Namko, and in 1962 while Rev. H. K. Lungalang was the Field Director, the 2nd edition of the Hymn book was produced by Miss. Heipei, Gaineu, Rev. Keneisie and others.[27] They are undeniably western hymnals with western tunes, yet these works led to the progress of the literature.

---

[24] The Lausanne Committee, "The Willowbank..." 498. The three self theorywas proposed in reaction to the mono-cultural mission export system, by Henry Venn and Rufus Anderson pioneer missionary thinkers, during the middle of the 19th century and Roland Allen in the early 20th century popularized the concept of "indigenous" churches, which would be "self-governing, self-supporting, and self-propagating."

[25] The Lausanne Committee, "The Willowbank..." 498.

[26] Suitei, *ZBCC...*, 85-86.

[27] Suitei, *ZBCC...*, 86.

3.4.2. The coming of Revival to the Zeliangrongs

It was as an outcome of the Revival that broke out in North America that Dr. Clark, bearing the seed of the gospel, came to North East India. He reached the Nagas superintending the mission field from Sibsagar in the early days.[28] The first wave of revival in Nagaland began in 1885 in Ao area where the church had already been planted in 1871-2. By 1913, the awakening vigorously spread and many Ao villages accepted the Christian faith.[29]

The second revival awakening took place in the 1950s across Nagaland and touched the Aos, the Lothas and the Angamis wherein the churches experienced the outpouring of the Holy Spirit. This was during the aftermath of the Second World War which threatened the Nagas with questions of spiritual security and agitated the hearts of the people so that the Christian influence became deeper.[30] The outcome of this revival made the Angamis more supportive of the evangelistic concept. Thus, the wind of the second revival awakening reached the Zeliangrong people along with the other tribes like the Kuki and the Rengmas.[31]

The third Revival Awakening in 1970s was more lasting and widespread in its effect in Nagaland[32] and in NEI. The Revival came to the Zeliangrong Nagas in the middle of 1976. This revival was like the blowing of wind or a burning flame which is beyond control. There was no particular person to say that s/he brought the Revival, but it can be rightly said that, God's spirit has visited the Zeliangrong people in a mighty way.[33] However, to trace its history, one can start with a crusade that was conducted at Peren Town Baptist church

---

[28] Phuveyi Dozo, *The Cross over Nagaland* (Guwahati: CLC, 1983), 8. Hereafter, Dozo, *The Cross over Nagaland*….

[29] Dozo, *The Cross over Nagaland*…, 8, 9. According to Rev. Rikhum, Nagaland Church came into being on the 23rd Dec. 1872. According to Clark's report, the revival began in 1885 and by 1889 revival progressed in Molung. As a result of the outbreak of the revival by 1897, the first Ao Association was conducted.

[30] Dozo, *The Cross over Nagaland*…, 15.

[31] Dozo, *The Cross over Nagaland*…, 18.

[32] Dozo, *The Cross over Nagaland*…, 19.

[33] Souvenir, *ZBAN*…, 27.

on 25th July 1976, and the movement of revival was seen from this crusade followed by other crusades and tours in the region. As a result of all these initiatives, the spirit of God began to work mightily in the region, touching all the Zeliangrong churches. The 1976 revival awakening is still continuing its work among the Zeliangrong churches.[34]

3.4.2.1. The impact of Revival Movement in 1970's

The revival awakening that came to the Zeliangrong people has brought many changes in the life of the society and the church. It has had both positive and negative impacts upon the people. It speeded up the conversion process and at the same time brought division in the church.

3.4.2.1.1. Negative impact

There were frequent preaching tours in big groups which affected the economic condition of the growing churches; there were also divisions of the church due to the conflict and confusion over the spiritual gifts. People began to neglect scripture and became enthusiastic about visions and prophecy.[35] The church leaders were given less regard as the people gave greater respect to those people who had spiritual gifts. Some believers went to the visionaries, as to practitioners of witchcraft in the past, to enquire about their problems and to know whether their sins were forgiven. Some people trusted more on those who had spiritual gifts than to the Doctors in the time of sickness.[36] Meanwhile, the Zeliangrong people had partially lost their cultural identity since the cultural values and practices were considered to be un-Christian, and much adaptation of western pattern took place as

---

[34] Souvenir, *ZBAN...*, 27, 28, 30. Again in the month of June and July 1977 a preaching group from Kohima Ao Baptist church toured the Zeliangrong area and many churches were enlivened. And in the same year on 25-28th August another Revival crusade was conducted at *Samziuram* Baptist Church by the Nagaland Missionary Movement. Another crusade was conducted in the month of October 1977 at Peren Town Baptist Church.

[35] Kiphuina, "A Study on the Impacts of Revival Movements among the Zeliangrong Naga"(B.D. thesis, Eastern Theological College, 2006), 54-55.

[36] Souvenir, *ZBAN...*, 28-29.

there was no proper guidance. According to Rev. Kuzierang Thou, it was the local visionaries who spoke against the traditional attires and dances as being dirty and devilish.[37] This could be due to the misjudgment, or wrong interpretation of the vision with their lack of deep and nuanced understanding of their own cultural context. In a way, they failed to study the vision in the light of the scripture, as the people began to believe more in visions and prophecy rather than the teachings found in the Bible.

3.4.2.1.2. Positive impacts

In the Zeliangrong region, the church was growing rapidly. In 1971, there were only 54 churches with 5,125 baptized members, but after the revival movement in 1981, the churches increased to 62 churches with 5,898 baptized members.[38] People did not get tired of reading the Bible, singing, praying and going to church every night. They had received joy and transformation, rededicated their lives to Christ and received both physical and spiritual healing. The believers received various spiritual gifts; ability to teach God's word, gift of prophesying, power of healing, gift of seeing visions, performing miracles and wisdom to differentiate between the good and the bad. As the joy of the people increased, the church's economic standing was also enhanced because the people sincerely gave tithes and free will contributions, and began to practice righteous living. More people went for theological training in search of the knowledge of God. Every activity began with prayer, and fasting also became popular. Anti-social activities were stopped and the people lived peacefully.[39]

3.4.2.1.2.1. *Zeranglei* and *Ketwalei*

During the aftermath of the revival movement, believers living in Peren, the headquarters of the Zeliangrong people in Nagaland who are also the members of the Peren Town Baptist Church formed a 'Prayer group' called *Kekiema*. They spent time praying and singing

[37] Interview with Kuzierang Thou, Executive Secretary, ordained minister of ZBCC, Peren Town, 9 October 2008. Hereafter Interview with Kuzierang...

[38] *BBC Centenary* ..., 48.

[39] Souvenir, *ZBAN*..., 27-28.

and through their inspiration from God, they had even compiled a revival song book known as *Zeranglei,* which was approved by the Zeme Christian Literature Committee, ZBCC.[40] Some songs are western hymns and some are the compositions of the local people. This song book is still used in the Sunday evening service, which is also called a revival service. *Ketwalei* are also sung by the Zeliangrong people as they emerge from a period of revival. Some of these songs also seem to come from the Hmar community. The first edition was prepared by Rev. Ngimrai in 1978.[41]

3.4.2.1.2.2. *Helim*

The Zeliangrong people sang revival songs and performed *helim* dances during the services, though the movements of the dancers were unorganized and non-uniform. However, by observing their dances and movements, one can monitor many similarities to their traditional dances, for example, raising of one's hand and waving above the heads, and various steps automatically taken by the feet according to the beating of the drums etc.[42]

3.4.2.1.2.3. Bible Translation

It was only after the revival movement among the Zeliangrong churches that the people gave more interest and time to read the Bible. However, the Bible was not available in the local dialect. Therefore, translation work was taken up by Rev. Visor H. Zeliang and the *Baibel Kehecibe,* the New Testament including Psalms and Proverbs, was completed and released on January 31st, 1981. After an interval of ten years the need to have a complete Bible was realized and the work began with the same translator and was completed under the supervision of the Bible Society of India on June 7, 1992.[43]

[40] *Zerang Lei* (Peren: ZBCC Literature Committee, nd.).

[41] Interview with Ngimrai, Ordained Pastor Jalukie 'B' Baptist Church, Jalukie, 31 Dec. 2008.

[42] Interview with Kerugai, Pastor and board of deacons of Samziuram Baptist Church, Samziuram, 18 October 2008.The other names for this same song book are *Twabeleu* and *Luisan.*

[43] Suitei, *ZBCC...,* 86. Heningkunglwa Baptist Church is one of the biggest and richest village churches under the ZBCC. She sponsored the translation of the

As time passed by, the church felt the need for a revision of the Bible and thus revision work began in the early 2000 (2001 or 2002) by the previous translator along with committee members, a trial copy of the revised Bible was printed out in the year 2013[44] and the correction work began in 2014.[45]

3.4.2.1.2.4. Re-edition of Hymn book

In 1973, the ZBCC released the Third edition of the Hymn Book called *Kerecalei,* mixing the Zeliangrong dialects as there was no common dialect for the kindred tribes. The fourth edition was done in 1986[46] and the fifth edition is going on at present. However, the work that is in progress is still very much based on western tunes and hymns.

3.5. Resurgence of traditional elements in Zeliangrong Christianity

Humans are created in the image of God, and by turn it is humans who create cultures, each containing many positive aspects that can be used by Christians. Every culture provides a measure of order that makes life meaningful and possible. A truly indigenous theology must be able to affirm the positive values of the culture in which it is being formulated.[47] Similarly, the Zeliangrong Churches have been making good use of the traditional and cultural things in their lives.

3.5.1. Traditional drum

Drums play a very important role in the life of Zeliangrong Christian worship today. A typical traditional Zeliangrong drum is made of hollow cylinder-shaped wood, naturally a trunk of a tree with animal skin stretched on both sides. The size of the drums used by the Zeliangrong people varies from community to community.

New Testament and the Translation of the Old Testament was sponsored byLamhai-Dungki Baptist Church which is another big village church under the ZBCC.

[44] Kemci Bible (Bangalore: The Bible Society of India, 2013) np.

[45] Izieteilung, telephone interview, 9 April 2018. The persons involved in the correction work are Rev. Kuzierang Thou, Rangro Herie and Izieteilung present ES.

[46] Suitei, *ZBCC...*, 86.

[47] Hiebert, *Anthropological Insights...*, 56.

Some drums are very big, such that a person cannot carry it alone, while some can be carried by one person and beaten while singing and dancing. The traditional society of the Zeliangrong people used drums very reverently.[48] The Zeliangrong people are a singing and dancing community, they sing and dance in most of the festivals, and in most of their singing the beating of a drum is necessary. Without a drum, they don't enjoy the songs and the dances. Thus, even when they are converted to Christianity they still continue to use the drums in their worship services; in fact, they prefer it over modern western musical instruments.

3.5.2. *Paupai rwaklei*

The *paupai rwaklei* are songs sung in traditional tunes with gospel lyrics. When the people, particularly the older generation, accepted the gospel and experienced salvation in their lives, they expressed their simple theology of joy and happiness of knowing the Lord through their self composed songs in the traditional tunes. One of the early converts of Benreu village Mr. Irialung, who was well known for his pietistic life, composed a song indicating his victory over the devils. His poem/song runs as follows:[49] 'Behold I have triumphed, I have bound the devil, even if I die today, I will inherit the eternal life, Go behind me Satan'. Likewise, many people composed songs from time to time but the churches do not appear to have seriously considered compiling these songs or including them in the church hymn books. According to Rev. Kuzierang Thou, composing songs and singing them to traditional tunes came to the surface only in the early 80s.[50] It is also said that the non-Christians seem to understand the words much better when the songs are sung in the traditional tunes rather than in the other tunes. So the songs in traditional tunes seem to

[48] In the Zeliangrong society, the Drum was very important; it was sacred and could not be used meaninglessly. The beating of a drum conveys warning, a sign for emergency, and a call for the people to be ready for the urgent situation

[49] Haisuitei, *A Historical Study…*, 23, cited *Benreu Baptist Church Diamond Jubilee Souvenir* (Benreu: BBCDJC, 1981), 15.

[50] Interview with Kuzierang…,Peren Town, 9 October 2008.

be a more effective to convey the message of the gospel to the non-Christians as they are more familiar with the tunes.[51]

3.5.3. Traditional attires

The Zeliangrong people are one of the richest people in their traditional attires among the Naga tribes.[52] The present Zeliangrong Christians, especially the women, are artistic and talented. Therefore, they wear different kinds of the traditional attires such as shawls and wraparound or *paitui*, as they go to church on Sunday for worship. Anyone can easily identify the beautiful and rich traditional attires of the Zeliangrong people by looking at their ladies in any ecclesiastical or social gatherings. They use their attires with great delight and use them in praise of God.

---

[51] Interview with Ileuheing, Field Evangelist ZBCC, Jalukie, 27th December 2008, Kwetranglu Pastor Azailong Baptist Church, Azailong, 11th October 2008 and Hedungziube a non-Christian leader, Ziumi, 3 January 2008. Ileuheing, who also had composed those songs and sang in his tours as an evangelist, and Mr. Kwetranglu Pastor expressed the same thing. Mr. Hedungziube was a non Christian man who said that the Christian songs are very hard to understand when sung in western tunes (now he is already converted to Christianity).

[52] Mirhu, "A Brief Account of Zeliangrong Nagas" (Manuscript prepared by Zeliangrong Students Union Assam Manipur and Nagaland, to be published in 2009), np. Hereafter, Mirhu, *A Brief Account....* The traditional Zeliangrong men wear Herampai and Njingai/Njingni from the waist to the knee. They wear shawls of different designs and colours, Nampame (white), Njingeo (black) and Mareipan, a white cotton cloth with the colourful stripes at the sides with embroidered pattern at the two tips, paimeu, langtapai, mleupai, Pheingao, Masin Pheipong. Other designs are Huram, Kaipai, HuTaron Changlon, Paban, and Maringmeiphei, Ngumthuakphai (shawl with a spear in the middle), Phaimiuphai, Lohephai, Tatiuni. The girls/ladies wear Taktui, Henipai and Npaimang. The formal shawls are Nphathik and Imphai, Pheisoi, Pheisoi and Nai, an undergarment for married women, and for elder women, Hu Bungting, Peo, Huchapei, Chepe, Pheisoi Hu. Ngumthuakphai (without spear), Nithuina, Langhiuphai, Langzinina, Tanina, Chakhenphai, Chalan (earring), Tatiu (necklace), Tata (bangles).

3.5.4. Traditional dances

The Zeliangrong people have three different forms of dances; ritual dances, festival dances and creative dances.[53] All these three variety of dances are incorporated in the Zeliangrong Christian worship life. The Zeliangrong Christians also participate in these dances during social functions. Sometimes, dances are performed and presented in the church functions especially by the experts as special items.

3.6. Cultural continuity among the Zeliangrong Christians

The ecclesiastical life of Zeliangrong Christians had a major weakness in that little to no effort was made from the church administration side to safeguard and promote their cultural practices and traditional elements in their lives due to the influence of the western customs and culture which the missionaries had imparted to most of the tribals. However, in spite of this, careful examination of the Zeliangrong Christian society today shows the reality that they still retain many cultural practices. In this regard, what Renthy Keitzar said is right; "Since the beginning of Christianity many of the customs and practices have been baptized and dyed into the local colour…Many of our customs and practices, for example, marriage and inheritance are retained without any change."[54] Thus, one can understand that the churches have already adapted to the local culture and practices in many ways. Below are some of the traditional elements which the Zeliangrong Christians still practice.

3.6.1. Rites connected with childbirth

The Zeliangrong welcomes the birth of a child. It is a matter of great joy, to parents and clansmen, neighbors and the whole village. When a child is born, normally a prayer of thanksgiving is offered for the safe delivery and the child is dedicated to the almighty *Tinggwang*. The naming of the child takes place usually five or more days after

---

[53] Mirhu, A brief Account…, n.p. 1) The ritual dances performed with great sacrifices during *Baanru, Taarang* and *Matui* festivals. 2) Festival dance performed during the festivals of the community. 3) Creative dances imitating nature and wildlife creatures, birds and insects.

[54] Renthy Keitzar, *Insearch of Relevant Gospel Message* (Guwahati: CLC, 1995), 52. Hereafter, Keitzar, *Insearch of Relevant…*

the birth. The name must be relevant to the lifestyle of the family; ambitious names are also given so as to encourage the child to live out a good life.

Consecration of a child is highly cherished by both the traditional Zeliangrong and the Christians. Even in the Scripture this act is found to be instituted by God. 'Initiating this rite is seriously taken in the Zeliangrong traditional practice, usually initiated by the mother who becomes the mediator between the child and the Supreme Being.'[55] This similar act of consecration is practiced by the present Zeliangrong Christians. Today a child is presented before God in the church just a few days after naming and is dedicated to God, initiated into the community by the pastor (minister), who gives thanks to God and offers a prayer of blessing upon the child and for a better future. After this act, the child is registered in the church and the child becomes an associate member in Christian community.

3.6.2. Marriage

Marriage is an elaborate ceremony among the Zeliangrong Christians though it does not entail much of the ritualistic performance anymore. Marriage between a very close relative has long been a taboo as it was not traditionally considered to be socially expedient.[56] Today, the degree of marriage relationship among the Zeliangrong is determined by certain social conditions. To initiate a marriage, the parents or relatives of the boy first approach the parents of the girl[57] and when both parties agree, marriage takes place at the appointed time. The practices of payment of the bride's price and slaughtering of animals still exist. Giving a particular portion of meat to the in-laws after the ceremonies is retained. All marriage ceremonial activities are initiated by the officially delegated Christian minister. One noteworthy custom which has been retained is the avoidance

---

[55] Iringtie Kauring, "Rites and Rituals of the Zeliangrong Nagas and its continuing Influence upon the Christians" (B.D. thesis, Eastern Theological College, 1999), 50. Hereafter cited as Iringtie, Rites and Rituals….

[56] S. T. Das, *Tribal Life in North East India* (Delhi: Gian Publishing House, 1986), 130.

[57] K. S. Singh ed., *People of India-Nagaland, Vol. XXXIV* (Calcutta: Naveen Kishore, 1994), 169.

of calling one's spouse by name. A newly-married couple avoids addressing each other by name as there is a surviving belief that to mention their spouse's name leads to the untimely death of either one of the two.[58]

3.6.3. Burial

Burial of the dead is also influenced by traditional practice.[59] Today, the Zeliangrong Christian funeral procedure is the same as practiced before in many ways. However, the entire committal acts are taken care of by the pastor or church elders. No sacrifice is offered but the family of the deceased kill animals to feed the friends, relatives and those who engaged themselves in voluntary works. Another manifestation is the practice of the erection of memorial stones for the dead.[60] Today, the Zeliangrong Christians erect memorial stones in a similar way; members of the bereaved family kill animals and invite their relatives and villagers to commemorate the erection of the stone. People gather in the house to pray. However, today one change is found in that the epitaph will now state the date of the person's acceptance of Jesus Christ, and the period of his/her service for the church can also be inscribed.[61]

3.6.4. House construction

Sacrifices were offered before the beginning of any construction work. It is because the land was believed to be inhabited by the spirits. The same belief is inherited by the Christians. Therefore,

---

[58] Iringtie, *Rites and Rituals...*, 50.

[59] The Zeliangrong considered the dead as one who goes on a long journey to the spiritual world. The dead are believed to be living in the land called *Heruiram*. Therefore, when a person died, the body was duly wrapped with a piece of cloth and placed inside the coffin along with the household articles which had been used by the dead during his/her lifetime. Things such as clothes, ornaments, spears and dao, were buried with the corpse, on the assumption that the dead could use them in the next world.

[60] Their forefathers erected stones in memory of the dead with sacrifices. Then the epitaph of the dead person was inscribed; mentioning the number of animals he killed, and the human heads he hunted in warfare.

[61] Iringtie, *Rites and Rituals...*, 51.

whenever they are to construct a new house at a new site, it is always preceded with a prayer for the sanctification of the site, so that no misfortune would fall upon the family. After the completion of the house it is traditionally retained that newly constructed houses must be dedicated to God. Hence, prayers are offered by the church elders for the protection of the home and family members against any devastation.[62]

3.6.5. Church Administration

The Zeliangrong society is a patriarchal society where the father is the head of the family and the men administrate the village in every sphere of life. The present Zeliangrong Christian society might have deeply ingrained this system of social order, so that even today there is not a single woman pastor, nor an ordained woman. However, the women enjoy enormous liberty in participating in the mission of God through the Women branch, which in many ways is even more effective than the general body of the church in terms of their financial position and contribution to mission work.

3.6.6. Influence of *keniu*

Ritual performance was always preceded or followed by strict observance of *keniu*. It is observed for the benefit of the individual's household, clans and village members of certain age groups. It is strictly observed.[63] Likewise, with the same sincerity and dedication, any Christian event, particularly Sunday, is solemnly observed by the Zeliangrong Christians. People abstain from journeying (unless it is unavoidable), playing certain games and sports, selling of any goods, animals or even the sale of things in the shops. This is done in the spirit of *genna*.[64]

---

[62] Iringtie, *Rites and Rituals…*, 52.

[63] *Keniu* is strictly maintained by abstaining from normal work and avoiding contact with the outside world. No goods and domestic animals are sold out from the village. If anyone violates this he/she is regarded to be in danger or sometimes a defaulter is served with severe action.

[64] Angeline, *The Nagas…*, 121.

3.6.7. Observances connected to cultivation

The festivals of the Zeliangrongs mark their agricultural activities. The traditional Zeliangrong people solely depend on cultivation; therefore the starting of their cultivation and ending of their harvest is taken seriously, reverently and observed in the form of *keniu.* For instance, sowing of the first seed *(heleu kai),* reaping of the first corn *(ludeu)* and completion of all the harvest and gathering *(baukaikap)* is accompanied by *keniu.* Even today the Zeliangrong Christians do not sow seeds without offering a prayer for the same, and they also observe a day set apart in the church calendar for "Thanksgiving" after the harvest is completed.[65]

3.6.8. Feast of merit

The traditional Feast of merit or *Kering Ga* was the usual practice of the rich people in the traditional Zeliangrong society where they offered their wealth for the whole community in the form of a feast, and many animals were slaughtered, with food and rice beer being offered in abundance. The Zeliangrong Christians have inherited the same and they do this in the form of hosting Christmas for the whole church and community. To cite an example, within 37 years' history of Ziumi Baptist Church, eight Christmas feasts had been hosted by various couples, widowers and widows.[66] Today, this is done in the spirit of Christian love and sharing with one another.

3.6.9. Slaughtering of animals

Slaughtering of animals was the means to communicate with the Supreme Being in the traditional Zeliangrong religious practice. Even today, there is no Christian occasion which is not accompanied

---

[65] This is usually observed towards the end of November, it is a day of gratitude to God for the rich harvest. On this day every family brings the first, fresh and best fruits to the church and offers it to God. This act of offering symbolizes their expression of Thanksgiving for the bountiful harvest. The offerings are collected and sold and the money used for God's service.

[66] Elungkiebe Zeliang, "A Reflection on Christmas Celebrations among the Tribal Christians of North East India," Journal of Tribal Studies 8/2 (July-December, 2004): 12. Ziumi Baptist Church is under Senapati district of Manipur, but it is a member of the ZBCC which is in Nagaland.

by feast and slaughtering of animals. They have inherited the traditional interest in their celebration of Christian occasions such as Christmas, Good Friday and Church Jubilees. As has been said, 'the present practice of lavish slaughtering of animals by the Zeliangrong Christian is not prescribed by the Scripture but acquired from the traditional sacrificial concepts.'[67]

3.7. Third Factor in the interaction of the Zeliangrong Christianity and culture: Modernization

Modernization is the joint offshoot of the British government and the Christian missionaries. With the Conquest of the Burmese in the first Anglo-Burmese war in 1823-26 the British started penetrating into Zeliangrong country in cooperation with the Raja of Manipur, and took over North Cachar, Assam, in 1839, establishing their headquarters at Asaloo. They entered the Naga Hills in 1866 and formed the Naga Hills district with the Headquarters at Samoogoodting.[68] Then in 1878 the British extended over to Kohima and Wokha and established their headquarters at Kohima

---

[67] Iringtie, *Rites and Rituals...*, 54.

[68] See A. Mackenzie, *The North-East Frontier of India* (Delhi: Mittal Publications, 1989), 145: Ramkhun, *The Zeliangrong...*, 9: Murkut Ramunny, *The World of Nagas* 2nd edition (New Delhi: Northern Book Centre, 1993), 8: Mirhu, *A Brief Account...* Chapter 4. Burma invaded and occupied Manipur for seven years (1819-1826). A prince of Manipur by the name Gambhir Singh, son of Bhagyachandra took help from the British and organized 500 soldiers. The Zeliangrong people of the area participated in the war of liberation against the Burmese. The British officers of Gambhir Singh, Manipur Levy, like Francis Jenkins, Gordon, Grant and Pamberton came into contact with the Zeliangrong people of Manipur and Naga Hills. The Anglo-Burmese war came to an end with the Treaty Yandabo in 1826. Gambhir Singh after his accession to the throne of Manipur carried out extensive expeditions against the Naga tribes like the Tangkhul, Poumai, Mao, Maram, Zeliangrong and the Angami in Manipur and Naga hills. This aggressive policy of Gambhir was fully backed by the British who provided soldiers, arms and ammunitions and money to Manipur levy whose members reached 3,000 after the Burmese war. Gambhir sent two expeditions to Naga villages in northern Manipur, and deep into the Angami hills after upgrading his army with the help of the British. In the winter of 1831, the first expedition was led by Raja Gambhir Singh with the Manipur levy under the command of Lt. Grant. Another expedition was led by Francis Jenkin's and R. B. Pamberton in 1832. The British had a tough fight with the Zeliangrong villagers

in 1882 with Deputy Commissioner in charge.[69] The Manipur sector of the Zeliangrong areas was brought under the British rule with their conquest of Manipur in 1891.[70] The British Imperialists after consolidating their rule in Kohima and surrounding Angami villages turned their attention towards the Barail ranges inhabited by the Zeliangs and succeeded in establishing their authority over the Zeliangrongs of Nagaland. With the Independence of India from British rule, Nagaland formally came within the Indian Union in 1947[71] and in 1963 Nagaland obtained statehood within the Indian Union. They then ushered in the election system in the state for the first time in January 10-16, 1964.[72]

3.7.1. Modernization under British Government

The British Government, for the extension and convenience of colonial administration, constructed a bridle path through Khonoma via Benreu to Tening outpost in 1885. Comfortable Dak Bangalows also known as Inspection Bangalows were constructed at Pedi, Peletkie and Tesangki.[73] There seems to have been a Primary School at Benreu Village in 1915;[74] this school must have been established under the British Government of India.

---

of Bapolongmai (Poilwa). Kohima (Thipommei to the Meitei) was also ransacked by Gambhir Singh.

[69] B. Pakem, *Coalition Politics in North East India* (New Delhi: Regency Publications, 1999), 115. Hereafter, Pakem, *Coalition Politics...*

[70] Achung Xavier, *Zeliangrong Movement...*, 13.

[71] Pakem, *Coalition Politics...*, 115. The Naga National Council under the leadership of A. Z. Phizo, declared Naga independence on 14th August 1947. The NNC was formed in 1946 having its origin in the District Tribal Council of 1945 as a body for the Nagas to decide their future after the transfer of British Power. This movement is also called the extremist group of the Naga Tribal Council; they continue to fight for the National freedom of the Nagas against the Indian Government till today. They are the mother of the existing Naga resistance movements that are still present in the state, such as, NSCN-IM, NSCN-K, NSCN-U. Meanwhile, the moderate group of the Naga Tribal Council worked with the India Union and obtained Statehood in 1963.

[72] Pakem, *Coalition Politics...*, 116.

[73] Peren, *Profile...*, 11.

[74] *BBC Centenary ...*, 11.

With the pending granting of political Independence to India during the early forties, the British Government ordered all the Naga tribes to form their own Tribal Councils. Accordingly, in acquiescence to this order the Zeliang-Kuki council was formed in 1943. Simultaneously with the formation of the Tribal Council, the leaders moved the Government for the recognization of Zeliang in lieu of 'Kacha Naga' and the same was conceded in 1944. Thus, the modern political system was introduced as a modern development against the ancient political systems of the Zeliangrong Nagas.

3.7.2. Modernization under free India

Peren Town was established in 1948 under the directive of the government administered by the local people. In 1958, Peren Town Headquarter was made as the first political administrative office for the area, which was upgraded to circle Administrative head in 1963, and became the office of the Sub-divisional officer (civil) in 1966. Finally, Peren Hqr. became a full-fledged District on 24th October, 2003.[75] It brought about many changes in the society such as a law and order system through the District Enforcement Force, the educational department, Health and Family welfare, electrification of the District through Department of Power, as well as a Public Health and Engineering Department.[76]

Transport and communication systems were improved, with the road from Kukidolong to Peren having been constructed in the 1950's.[77] Tele-communication systems such as radio, television, telephone, computer, mobile, and the internet reached to the Zeliangrong people, which greatly influenced their mindset and

[75] Peren, *Profile...*, 15.

[76] Peren, *Profile...*, 20-22. DEF Superintendent of Police Peren Hq. was established on August 10, 1993. Education Dept. is headed by the Deputy Inspector of schools, Peren Hq. Estd. in March 31. 1979. Health & Family Welfare Dept. in the district is headed by the SDMO Peren, Estd. in April 1980. Public and Engineering Department was Estd. in 1997.

[77] Interview with Mr. Suigong Pame, A Government School Teacher, Peren Town, 9th March 2009.

worldviews.[78] An easier life was ushered in and accordingly these lifestyle changes led them to discard their traditional heritages; their value of a communitarian lifestyle was slowly replaced by the individualistic lifestyle.

3.7.3. Modernization through Christian missionaries

It was in 1872 that the American Baptist Mission started the mission work among the Nagas. Along with Christianity, a new worldview made up of western culture, politics, science, technology, medicines, schools and literature was introduced to the tribals.[79] The most important mode of modernization of the tribal society was the development of literature. Missionaries transcribed the tribal dialects to writing by introducing the Roman script, followed by translations of hymns and scriptures. Through the introduction of literature, a new tribal identity emerged, as various dialects of tribals were reduced to a script which was learned by the whole tribe thereby providing a common linguistic medium and unity to the tribals.[80] Thus, Christianity created a new sense of tribal identity; which later became the basis of modern political movements.

The introduction of education by the missionaries ushered in modernization to the tribals. It is interesting to note that wherever a church was founded, a school was also established simultaneously by the early missionaries. These schools were popularly known as Mission Schools. For instance, in 1884 C. D. King had started a mission school at Kohima.[81] After India's Independence, the educational programme was taken over by the Government or merged with the Government-run schools. However, the Mission

---

[78] Mr. Suigong assumes that television began to be used by the Zeliangrong people in the late 1980s, telephone in the early 1990s, and mobile cellphones in early 2005.

[79] A. Wati Longchar, *The Tribal Religious Traditions in North East India; An Introduction,* Revised ed. (Jorhat: Published by the Author, 2000), 141.

[80] F. S. Downs. *History of Christianity in India, Vol. 1, Part 5* (Bangalore: CHAI, 1992), 192-93.

[81] Bareh, *Gazzeetter of India…,* 193.

Schools became the nurseries for change as the peoples assimilated new faith and also learnt about science, politics and technology.[82]

In the case of the Zeliangrong Christians, they have only indirect benefits, as the foreign missionaries did not come directly and establish schools in their area and transcribe their dialect into script. It was the Zeliangrong people who went and studied from the Mission Schools, so the influence was still significant. The influence could be seen in the Mission Schools established by the Zeliangrong Baptist Churches. The curriculum and administration were almost an exact duplication of the missionaries' Mission Schools. As such, the Zeliangrong missionaries have given much importance to the study of the Holy Bible and Christian doctrines in the school education, without ignoring other academic subjects in the school curricula, like simple Arithmetic, English primers, History and even some basic knowledge about elementary science.[83] The medium of learning is also in English. Today, these Mission Schools are on a par with if not better than the Government-run Schools, providing modern education for the students. As the Zeliangrong people are educated and became literate, they are more exposed to the modern world.

Conclusion

The above discussion has highlighted the encounter between the Zeliangrong culture and Christianity, along with the influence of modernity. The influence of Zeliangrong culture on Zeliangrong Christians was not significant in the first period but the influence of the modernity was quite high both in secular and religious life, that is, when they were under the control of the missionaries or the Kohima Mission Field. The best they could do for indigenization of Christianity during this period was the translation of the hymns in local dialect. Another factor for the weak relationship between gospel and culture was the persecution faced by the early converts from their own kinsmen who held on to traditional faith and the followers

[82] Longchar, *The Tribal Religious Traditions*...142.

[83] O. L. Snaitang, "Christian Mission and Social Transformation in North East India" *Mission in Context: Missiological Reflections Essays in Honour of Roger and June Hedlund*. C. V. Mathew, ed., (Delhi: DMIIS/ISPCK, 2003), 31.

of the *Heraka* cult. This discouraged early converts from holding on to their traditional practices.

But in the second period (1953 onwards) modernity took hold of the social life of the people, but significant progress was made in indigenizing Christianity. The 1970s revival awakening had a remarkable impact on the lives of the Zeliangrong people as many were converted to Christianity. Thanks to the revival movement, there is now a good deal of cultural continuity in the life of the Zeliangrong Christians that has been inherited from the traditional practices; in fact this marks their identity. Thus, one can see that the Christianity which came from the west and the modernity brought by the British and the Government of India and Nagaland state government superficially appeared to have affected their traditional way of life and their worship of the Supreme Being, but it did not do away with the whole cultural and traditional way of life. As such, the Zeliangrong Christians did not totally abandon their traditional way of life.

Chapter 4

PRESENT ZELIANGRONG CHRISTIANITY AND MISSION: CHALLENGES OF IDENTITY

Introduction

Having described the account of the encounter between the traditional Zeliangrong society and Christianity, we shall now more elaborately examine the state of the present Zeliangrong Christian society. Judging from the Benreu Baptist Church Centenary celebration record,[1] the Zeliangrong churches have grown significantly over the past 120 years. In this chapter we shall look into the outcome of the interaction between the Zeliangrong cultural life and Christianity, in the light of Richard Niebuhr's discussion on the relationship between Christ and culture, with more emphasis on the impact of the Zeliangrong tradition and culture on the Zeliangrong Christians. Then we shall also examine the mission activities of the Zeliangrong Baptist Associations.

[1] BBC, *Centenary...*, 19-20.

4.1. H. Richard Niebuhr's Propositions

Niebuhr understood culture as the total process of human activity.[2] For him Culture is the "artificial, secondary environment" which man superimposes on the natural. It comprises of language, habits, ideas, beliefs, customs, social organization, inherited artifacts, technical processes, and values. He identifies that "social heritage," which is what the New Testament writers frequently had in mind when they spoke of "the world," has many forms and it was to this that Christians like other humans are inevitably subject.

Furthermore, Niebuhr says that culture is a human achievement. He says that culture is the work of human minds and hands. It is the portion of human heritage in any place or time given designedly and laboriously by our predecessors. It includes speech, education, myth, science, art, philosophy, government, law, rites, beliefs, inventions, technologies. He also said that the world of culture is a world of values. What humans have made and what they make is intended for a purpose; it is designed to serve a good. So in short Niebuhr understood culture in its whole dimension, as the whole activities of humankind, in which modernization is included. Niebuhr goes on to discuss the relationship between Christ and culture through different propositions.

4.1.1. Christ against Culture

The first is '*Christ against culture.*'[3] It implies that Christ is the only authority and the claim of culture to authority is to be rejected. The counterpart of loyalty to Christ is the rejection of cultural society. A supporting Scripture passage for this approach is found in the injunction to Christians, 'Do not love the world or the things in the world. If anyone loves the world, love for the father is not in him'. The 'world' appears as a realm under the power of evil into which the children of God should not enter. This proposition is provocative and factional in nature. It repudiates the surrounding culture as evil and separates the Christian from the world.[4] This religious

[2] Niebuhr, *Christ and Culture…*, 32-34.

[3] Niebuhr, *Christ and Culture…*, 47-48.

[4] Niebuhr, *Christ and Culture…*, 45-46.

understanding continues to be stringently emphasized by many imperial and exclusive minded persons among the Zeliangrong. People subscribing to such a view make a very selective choice of traditional cultural elements; they reject anything which does not conform to the official missionary ethos.

4.1.2. Christ of Culture

The second proposition is *'Christ of Culture'* which means Jesus is the Messiah of cultures.[5] Christians who hold onto this thought form do not feel any great tension between the church and the world, the social laws and the gospel. On the one hand they interpret culture through Christ; on the other hand they understand Christ through culture. They do not ignore or neglect this-worldly or other-worldly views. They attempt to follow Christ without abandoning important cultural practices healthy for the society. In this model we don't see conflict between Christ and culture. It affirms Christ as the fulfillment of culture. 'Culture-Protestantism' in 19th century Germany is a typical example.[6] This position is identifiable in the theology of C.S. Song where enfleshment and God's identification with humanity is depicted as a model.[7] But Song is careful enough to avoid simplistic reductionism; to put the whole intricacy of Christianity and culture in juxtaposition. There have been similar voices from some intellectual and conscious members in the church to infuse this religiosity; which weighs Christ and culture equally. An analogous position is suggested by Horam, 'to remain a good Christian at the same time living as a good Naga,' where reciprocal interaction or fusion of the cultural horizon will serve a complementary outcome.[8]

---

[5] Niebuhr, *Christ and Culture…*, 83-85.

[6] Niebuhr, *Christ and Culture…*, 91-101.

[7] C.S. Song, *Third-Eye Theology* (New York: Orbis Book, 1979), 184.

[8] M. Horam, *Nagas Old Way New* Trends (New Delhi: Cosmo Publications, 1988), 57.

4.1.3. Christ above Culture

The third Proposition is *Christ above Culture.*[9] It means that the reception of grace perfects and completes culture though there is not a smooth curve or continuous line between them. This position affirms a synthesis of Christ and culture. In it Christianity neither rejects nor affirms culture. In contrast, it transcends culture.[10] Renthy Keithzar, a pioneer of Tribal Theology, proposed this hermeneutical approach where Christ is looked upon as the Victor over the spirit and also the fulfiller of the culture.[11] It asserts that Christianity supersedes traditional religion or ethical teachings, though there are some good elements in traditional culture. This concept can also be found in the theology of Thanzauva, a renowned tribal theologian who cautions against 'culturalism' in which culture is venerated and romanticized above the Bible.[12]

4.1.4. Christ and Culture in Paradox

The fourth proposition is *Christ and culture in Paradox,*[13] meaning both are authorities to be obeyed and the believers live within this tension. This position postulates Christ and culture side by side. It creates two conceptual realms; Christ within the spiritual realm and culture within the earthly realm.[14] Yet both make their demands on humans. The Japanese theologian Onish exemplified this paradox when he promulgated that the love for God and the respect for the emperor could exist side by side, for the political authorities were instituted by God.[15] This notion is also an important theological

---

[9] Niebuhr, *Christ and Culture...*, 119.

[10] Niebuhr, *Christ and Culture,* 128-141.

[11] Keitzar, *In Search of a Relevant...*, 23.

[12] K. Thanzauva, *Theology of Community: Tribal Theology in the Making* (Aizawl: Mizo Theological Conference, 1997), 87. Hereafter Thanzauva, *Theology of Community...*

[13] Niebuhr, *Christ and Culture...*, 149.

[14] Niebuhr, *Christ and Culture,* 208.

[15] Cited by Takaaki Haraguchi, "Reflections on H. Richard Niebuhr's Theoretical Model Concerning the Relationship between Christianity and Culture: Its Applicability to the Japanese Context," in *Asia Journal of Theology,* Vol. 21, No. 2 (October 2007), 234.

principle in the two kingdom theories of St. Augustine and Martin Luther, for example.

4.1.5. Christ the Transformer of Culture

The fifth propositionis '*Christ the Transformer of culture*'.[16] Culture reflects the fallen state of humanity; in Christ, humanity is redeemed and culture can be renewed so as to glorify God and promote his purposes. It supports Christians to engage in world affairs and to transform the culture of the world.[17] Along this religious footprint Thanzauva writes, 'in this process both Christianity and tribal culture are mutually reshaped and transformed.'[18]

In the light of Niebuhr's propositions when we look into the encounter of the Zeliangrong cultures with Christianity we could see that almost all the propositions of Niebuhr have taken place in one or the other form and this creates more problems and tensions regarding their identity.

4.2. Looking at the Present State of Zeliangrong Christians through Niebuhr's Propositions

The home of the Zeliangrong, Peren District has an area of 2,300 sq. km. with a total population of 96,825 in which 95% are said to be Christians. Dominated by the Baptist denominational tradition, there are also various other denominations in the district.[19] Comparatively only a very few members of the population are holding on to the traditional religion and some 3,000 of them are holding on to the reformed Zeliangrong *Heraka* cult.[20] As one examines the nature of Zeliangrong Christianity one discerns the operation of the propositions of Niebuhr:

---

[16] Niebuhr, *Christ and Culture…,* 190, 194.

[17] Neibuhr, *Christ and Culture,* 209.

[18] Thanzauva, *Theology of Community…,* 89.

[19] Peren, *Profile…,* 11.

[20] Interview with Aninge Mariam, Headmistress, Zeliangrong Heraka School, Tening, 16 October, 2008.

4.2.1. Christ against culture

Some Zeliangrong Christians who oppose the traditional practices and customs take a firm stand on the first proposition of Niebhur's *'Christ Against culture.'*[21] This proposition is in agreement with the Lausanne Committee statement which states that, "the most outstanding thing about a Christian should not be his/her culture, but his/her Christ-likeness."[22] Such Christians among the Zeliangrong strongly asserts that they have forsaken their traditional practices like their songs and dances, attires and ornaments, because they feel that they are bad as they are associated with pride or romance and they fear that reviving them will cause more harm to the people and society, which may even lead to barren Christian living.[23] However, this group was represented by only a few people. In this regard a question was asked in a questionnaire, "Christianity is better than our culture and tradition; so is it alright to forsake our culture and traditions?" To this 8.6% answered "Yes" and the rest 91.4% answered "No." This shows that only a few representatives of the Zeliangrong Christians are taking the stance of Christ against culture.

4.2.2. The Christ of Culture, Christ above Culture, and Christ the Transformer of Culture

These three propositions of Niebhur's *Christ and Culture* are very closely associated in the thought form of the Zeliangrong Christians.

---

[21] Niebuhr, *Christ and Culture...*, 47-48.

[22] *Willowbank Report...*, 504. Christ is the Lord of the universe and the church; he is Lord of the individual believer also. We find ourselves gripped by the love of Christ. It hems us in and leaves us no escape. Because we enjoy newness of life through his death for us, we have no alternative but to live for him who died for us and rose again (2 Cor. 5:14, 15). Our first loyalty is to him, to seek to please him. His necessitates the renunciation of all lesser loyalties. So we are forbidden to conform ourselves to this world's standards, that is, to any prevailing culture which fails to honour God, and are commanded instead to be transformed in our conduct by renewed minds which perceive the will of God. God's will was perfectly obeyed by Jesus. Therefore, "the most outstanding thing about a Christian should not be his/her culture, but his/her Christ likeness."

[23] Interview with Mr. Peida Nza, a member of prayer group which is the product of 1970s revival movement in Zeliangrong region. Peren Town, 9 September 2008.

Through God's grace human cultures were perfected and thus find their fulfillment in Christ, resulting in transformation of culture and society.

Christ of culture is modeled in the influence of *keniu* (ritual rest) which finds its fulfillment on Sunday, as it is observed in the spirit of *keniu*, as a day of complete rest. The traditional festivals with their feasting have also found their place in Christian festivals like Christmas, Good Friday and Easter, as they are celebrated in special ways in the spirit of traditional feasting, making it memorable for all the members. Everyone looks forward to these important events with the same anticipation as might have been reserved for traditional feasts.

Christ above Culture in the Zeliangrong Christian society can be seen firstly, in their proposal for marriage wherein they still follow the traditional system, the bride price and the kind of relationships established for the young woman with her brothers, cousins and uncles.[24] Again the clan, kin and kith relationship are strictly observed by the Zeliangrong Christians. However, they now accept the gospel imperative for Christians to love one another, not only our near and dear ones, but also one's enemies. This makes the scope of love greater and wider, and shows *Christ above Culture* in action in the life of the Zeliangrong Christians.

Some examples for *Christ the Transformer of Culture* are; the cultural practice of headhunting was replaced by love for every human soul. The psycho-political consciousness of an exclusive and independent mindset was transformed and changed to embrace a wider and open community. There has also been transformation of the socio-cultural separation of men and women into an integrated culture, especially by replacing the *Morung* (*Hangsiuki-* boys' dormitories, *Liusiuki-* girls dormitories) system and introducing church and schools where both the genders gather together.

[24] The bride's price will be distributed among those brothers, cousins and uncles whom the bride's father chooses from his kinsmen to have a special relationship with the young married woman in order to help and share with each other in every circumstance of life.

4.2.3. Christ and culture in paradox

In the Zeliangrong traditional culture, a man is permitted to divorce his wife if she is issueless and unable to bear a child, but in the Christian teaching a couple has to live together 'till death; there is no grounds for divorce. Drinking of rice beer (wine) is the nourishing drink for the Zeliangrong people but Christian doctrines do not permit drinking of wine. The church takes disciplinary action against those who drink. Politics is a part of the culture today, but the church does not approve churchmen involving in party politics. In all these cases there is a tension for the Zeliangrong Christians as to how they should go about their lives.

4.3. Confused Identity in the face of modernity

In Niebuhr's *Christ and Culture,* he related everything about culture to human life. Though he did not make direct reference to modernity, modernity is included within culture. In this regard, the present Zeliangrong society is at a crossroads caught between modernity (offshoot of Christian mission and the British government initially and later on the Indian Government) and tradition, unable to creatively integrate the two in their lives. In other words, it is difficult to navigate their transformation from a society that lived in isolation amid unique tribal set-ups in the deep mountainous forests of the Naga Hills, to their present world of international communication and satellite television.[25] The society on one hand is still in the pre-industrial or primitive agricultural age, but on the other hand it is enjoying the benefits of the latest inventions. This leads to the reckless selling of their assets, mainly natural resources and land, leading to an identity crisis.

The question of identity has become a problem for the Zeliangrong people, particularly to the younger generation, due to the influence of modernization through education brought about by the joint forces of the British government and the Christian mission initially and later on by the Indian government and state

---

[25] Angeline Lotsüro, *The Nagas…,* 172, citing "At crossroads: Nagas in Transition on the Threshold of the 21st Century," *The North East Age,* 276 November, 1997, p. 9.

government and the local churches.[26] The blessings of the educational institutions of the missionaries also reached the Zeliangrong people as they accepted the Christian faith, though no missionary had opened a mission school in the Zeliangrong areas. The expansion of educational institutions at various levels, from primary school to university level, enhance the quality of life for many, but it also generates gaps in the society. M. Alemchiba has rightly said that, "… an 'uneasy population' unable to adjust themselves with village life was created in the rural population."[27] Consequently, many of the things which were valued in the traditional society were ignored and discarded.

The younger generation of the Nagas are the worst affected group. The craze for the latest gadgets without rooting themselves in the firm anchor of tradition and culture has made them lose their sense of identity. "They were neither the traditional Nagas nor can they really be their counterparts, even though they may dress like them and sing their songs as well as they can."[28] As a result there is a vacuum in the lives of many Naga youth. This void and emptiness is being filled with the use and abuse of drugs, alcohol and other social evils. There are no social institutions like *Hangsiuki* where the youth are trained in the traditions and culture of the tribe. Many parents and elders could no longer have any influence on the youth today as the youth are more educated and better informed than the older citizens. Thus, we see the failures of the Zeliangrong society in resolving the tensions between the old traditions, the new culture and the Christian faith.

In a situation like this, to know the Zeliangrongs' self perception of their Christianity, in the questionnaire a question was put forward, "Are the present Zeliangrongs devoted in their Christian living like their foreparents?" Sadly only 11.4% responded positively

---

[26] Angeline, *The Nagas…*, 97. Early missionaries like Clark, Downs Supplees, C. D. King, Rivenburge and William Pettigrew made great efforts to establish schools and gave education to the Nagas.

[27] M. Alemchiba, "Problems of Re-adjustment to a New Situation (with special reference to the Naga tribes)," In K. S. Singh, ed., *Tribal Situation in India* (Shimla: Indian Institute of Advanced Study, 1972), 483.

[28] Angeline, *The Nagas…*, 173.

expressing that true Christians are really devoted, but the remaining 88.6% gave a negative response that they were not satisfied with the present Zeliangrong Christianity. In the words of some scholars, the present state of the Zeliangrong Christianity can be termed as skin deep and shallow Christianity.[29] This is seen in their present society as there are rampant evils of alcoholism and substance abuse, resulting in the breaking up of families. The present study shows that this may be because of the failure to indigenize the Christian faith into their culture and integrate their culture into their Christianity and contextualize their Christianity, and also due to lack of relevant faith formation.

4.4. Looking at the Mission of the Zeliangrong Baptist Church Associations (ZBCAs)[30] through Niebuhr's Propositions

With the acceptance of the gospel and their conversion to Christian faith, the Zeliangrong experienced love, joy, freedom, happiness, and salvation through Christ. As a result they actively got involved in mission work. From the very initial stage of the church the mission work was carried out mainly by the native people among her own citizens through the means of preaching. In our deliberation we shall see how successful or unsuccessful they were in their mission activities in making Christianity relevant to their culture and context. Even as Niebuhr understood culture as the total process of human activity, in the following discussion culture includes both the traditional heritage and the things that pertain to modernity.

4.4.1. Christ against culture

One of the first methods of spreading the gospel is evangelism. Lindsell asserts that "one tried and proved method for spreading the gospel is evangelism, it is the heart of all methods and indeed must

---

[29] See Jesudas M. Athyal, ed., *Relevant Patterns of Christian Witness in India: People as Agents of Mission, Mission – Evangelism Studies, Vol. I* (Thiruvalla: Christava Sahithya Samithy and Mission-Evangelism Study Project, 2000), 84; Angeline, *The Nagas...*, 177.

[30] The Mission work of the ZBCAs is provided in the Appendix.

be kept central in any of them."[31] The second coming of Christ is one of the strongest motifs of evangelism for the Zeliangrong Christians. They held onto the belief that this material world is coming to an end, all materials will be destroyed, but only those who believe in Christ will be saved.[32] They were against culture, or at the very least they were not cautious of the importance of culture, and its relevancy in their mission activities.

Church planting is another common practice; wherever the missionaries or evangelists go, new converts are organized into a fellowship and then a local church. From the very beginning, the early Zeliangrong Christians were active in converting and planting churches. However, their churches were not really indigenous. Both in terms of physical forms and in its administration system, they are still a legacy of the 19th century evangelical American Christianity.[33] The attempt to indigenize Christianity was very minimal, since both the missionaries and the early local converts did not make much effort towards it; the same attitude is inherited by the present Christians. This mindset of the people needs to be changed. Ironically, the wealth of poetical songs and the beauty of traditional festivities were shunned by the early Zeliangrong Christians. This heritage was rejected as part of the 'old' paganistic tradition.[34] Thus, even today the traditional poetical tunes and the festivities have very little place in the life of the Zeliangrong Churches. The Zeliangrong ecclesiastical life is very faithful to the western Christian tradition.

The ZBCAs also encourages music ministry in the churches, by organizing and producing audio cassettes, conducting music trainings and music camps, and also organizing music festivals. However, any attempt for reviving indigenous music and tunes is hardly seen and the inherited mindset towards traditional tunes and

---

[31] Harold Lindsell, *Missionary Principles and Practices* (West Wood, New Jersey: Fleming H. Revell Company, 1954), 191.

[32] Wati Longchar, *The Traditional Tribal Worldview and Modernity; Focus on North East India,* (Jorhat: N. Limala Lkr, Eastern Theological College, 1995), 136. Hereafter, Longchar, *Traditional Tribal...*

[33] Keitzar, *Insearch of Relevant...*, 19.

[34] Lalsangkima Pachuau, *Ethnic Identity and Christianity* (Frankfurt am Main: PeterLang, 2002), 132.

music as being devilish and taboo is still very fresh in the mind of some people. Even today the indigenous tunes do not have a place in the Zeliangrong church hymn books. The educational mission also reflects this framework as they emphasize only the western oriented education with some emphasis on Christian faith. One can scarcely see the efforts to impart traditional values to the students.

The people understand politics to be dirty and the churches do not encourage party politics but people can hardly abstain from politics. As a result, corruption prevails. Most of the party workers become insincere to the church as there is a dividing line between religion and politics which is a part of today's culture. Sadly, even some church deacons tendered their resignation to the church to contest in the Town Council election in 2008.

4.4.2. Christ and culture in Paradox

The traditional customary law emphasizes the strict maintaining of communitarian life, but Christianity teaches personal piety and individual salvation. While Christianity holds the world to be sinful and temporary, traditional worldview holds the world as sacred.[35] The Zeliangrong society is a patriarchal society where aged men are given more importance and respect in the society. Churches with this patriarchal mindset have a rigid resistance to women and bachelors entering into pastoral and ordained ministry, and leadership in the church was preferably given to elderly men. But Christian participation in God's mission demands all people, both men and women, young and old, to enter into full-time ministry and actively work in various capacities. So in all these cases we see the tension between gospel and culture.

4.4.3. Christ of culture

Literature work undertaken as a part of mission activities is a must for proclaiming the gospel. One of the biggest projects of the ZBCAs is Bible translation, and all the four Associations have a Bible and Hymn book in their own local dialect. Important journals like

---

[35] A. Wati Longchar, *The Tribal Religious Traditions in North East India: An Introduction* (Jorhat: Author, 2000), 147.

Samlia and *Chailihei* are published regularly in local dialects.[36] The Indigenous mission limits itself to the same dialect group, and is carried out by the local people by making use of the local resources; it is a mission which is at its best a way of self-governing, self supporting and self proclaiming. This activity develops their identity through developing their literature. It is through Christ that the local dialect which is a part of culture got its fulfillment, and it is clear that the indigenous mission helped her maintained her identity.

The resurgence of traditional elements like songs in indigenous tunes and dances which were once abandoned are slowly developing among the Zeliangrong Christians today and hopefully they will be soon incorporated into Christian Hymns and have their prominent place in the life of the Zeliangrong Christians society.

4.4.4. Christ above culture

Gospel camps and crusades are other important tools for evangelism, being used by the Zeliangrong evangelists, missionaries and churches in their mission endeavors to strengthen one's spiritual life and also to win over the non-Christians. Though this incurs heavy expenses, it proves helpful in sharing the gospel and winning more souls.[37] The ZBCAs mission work in partnership with other organizations and associations of other tribes and her outreach mission to other communities means they can situate themselves well in this framework. These activities neither reject nor affirm culture, but give importance to God's mission alone. In this regards one of the evangelists said, the best method for evangelism is to live a good life and be friends with the non Christians so that we can impart the gospel when they are on good terms with us.[38] Likewise another

[36] *Samlia* is the Zeme Baptist Church council's Bulletin, and *Cailihei* is a theological journal.

[37] *ZBCC Samlia Vol. 5...*, 14, 15. Gaili Baptist Church pastor reports of a Gospel Camp conducted in his church on 11th – 13th July 2008. He stated that 5persons took water baptism, 24 persons were restored back to the church and 89 persons rededicated themselves for the service of the Lord. Mr. Diteibui Church Secretary of New Puilo Baptist Church also reported the great success of the Home Crusade program.

[38] Interview with Kusa, Evangelist, Ngwalwa Town, 15 October, 2008.

evangelist also said that home visitation is an important method for evangelism, because we can call more people to Christ by sharing the gospel and sharing our love.[39]

4.4.5. Christ the Transformer of culture

Three Associations, namely LBA, ZBA and ZBCC, out of four Zeliangrong Baptist Church Associations, have established Schools managed by the associations. The local churches also establish mission schools as a part of their mission. Through this educational mission there were many transformations taken place in the Zeliangrong society; firstly, students were taught to live a hygienic life, they become literate and they were exposed to other peoples in the wider world. Secondly, education helped to promote a new social relationship among the Zeliangrong people, thus, their tribal identity and unity was strengthened.

Conclusion

As we have seen in the above discussion, today the Zeliangrong society is a Christian society though their Christianity is shallow and skin deep as they themselves have acknowledged. Despite the cultural continuity found in their lives, the influence of the contemporary world has been so strong that there is confusion of their identity. However, the good thing is that about 90% of the respondents of the Zeliangrong Christians want to revitalize the good cultural elements in their lives and also incorporate the healthy elements of the contemporary world in their lives.[40] This has to be encouraged by the churches so as to let the people root themselves deep into their culture and also be dynamic in the present society. The Zeliangrong Christians have great zeal to participate in the mission work and mission activity remains as active as it was in the beginning. Yet there are no properly planned strategies, which is the basic need for the churches today to be more effective and relevant to the culture and context. The century old mission strategy that sent evangelists for

---

[39] Interview with Ihecing, Evangelist, Gaili, 14 October, 2008.

[40] The question was, 'Will it be good to incorporate good elements from the traditional culture values in our Christian lives?'

mission work has to be changed and a system that would be more effective, enhancing and relevant for today's context and the culture and the identity of the Zeliangrong people must be innovated. Therefore, the next chapter discusses on "Towards a meaningful Indigenous Zeliangrong Christianity and a Relevant Contextual Mission".

Chapter 5

TOWARDS A MEANINGFUL INDIGENOUS ZELIANGRONG CHRISTIANITY AND RELEVANT CONTEXTUAL MISSION

Introduction

Having discussed about the Zeliangrong Christians and the mission activities taken up by the ZBCAs, with reference to Richard Niebuhr's five propositions, we have been enabled to analyze the encounter and interaction between Gospel and culture in the foregoing chapter. However, his framework does not equip us to respond to the contextual understanding of the relationship between culture and gospel because Niebuhr does not attempt to propose any device for his readers to follow in their attempt to indigenize Christianity in their culture and contextualize Christianity to their contexts. So his propositions, useful as they are, are not adequate enough for our purpose here. Therefore, we rather prefer an integrative and constructive fusion of Culture and Gospel in order to call for a meaningful indigenous Zeliangrong Christianity and for a vibrant and relevant contextual mission. To reach this end we will be using a framework which will integrate Christian faith, culture and modernity. This chapter in the first place discusses what Indigenous Zeliangrong Christianity means and secondly proposes some mission strategies in the light of the proposed framework, which would be culturally and contextually relevant.

5.1. Indigenous Zeliangrong Christianity

Brahmabandhav Uphadhyay perceived himself to be a "Hindu-Catholic."[1] He made a distinction between "*Samaj dharma* and *Sadhana dharma*"; as per the former he was a Hindu and as per the latter he was a Christian.[2] In the same manner, Indigenous Zeliangrong Christians would be persons who are Christians by faith and Zeliangrong by culture, being faithful to both and living accordingly without forsaking one at the expense of the other. Hence, the task ahead for the Zeliangrong Christians is to make the Zeliangrong people genuine Zeliangrong Christians.

Culture is dynamic; it grows and changes as it interfaces with other cultures. So the Zeliangrong culture has been going through this same process of change and developments through interaction with other cultures. However, meaningful Indigenous Zeliangrong Christianity does not imply exclusive faithfulness to the old Zeliangrong cultures of the past. It should be an existential reality of theological interpretation of Christian truth in terms of Zeliangrong culture and our way of life of the past, present and future. To reach this end the church needs to have a mission which is relevant to the context and culture of the people and this mission has to be done by all sections of Zeliangrong people by uplifting one another, considering and taking every aspect of life seriously.

5.2. Integration of Christian faith, culture and modernity

The Zeliangrong Christians hold that all their cultural practices and all the things of modernity are not bad. There are some good and liberating elements, though at the same time all are not good. Things

---

[1] Evelyn Monteiro, *Church and Culture: Communion in Pluralism* (Delhi: ISPCK, 2004), 131.

[2] K. P. Aleaz, *The Gospel of Indian Culture* (Calcutta: Punthi Pustak, 1994), 231. *Samaj dharma* refers to living manners, customs, eating and dressing based on the observance of the caste system, since he was a Hindu by culture. However, as per spiritual practices (*Sadhana)* and the quest for the experience of salvation (*Mukti),* he was a Christian.

which will be invigorative for Christian living should be accepted and rejuvenated. The good and enlivening elements in both the cultural practices and things in modernity should be sustained; the unclean elements should be made clean if not rejected, or invested with Christian meanings and used in Christian living to produce genuine Christians. 75% of the respondents were not satisfied with the present trend of mission and their answers suggest a mission strategy similar to this framework.[3] Some of the interviewees said that many of the Zeliangrong cultural practices are just the same with the biblical culture; the only difference in Christianity is to believe in Christ and to get baptism in his name to be saved.[4] Another person said that traditional culture is better in its own way for the society because it gives immediate punishments for the culprits in a way that is not found in Christian religion.[5] Old customs can be given new symbolism, old dances can celebrate new blessings, and old crafts can serve new purposes. To borrow an Old Testament expression, swords can be hammered into pruning knives.[6] However, the destructive and unhealthy cultural elements which cannot be transformed should be discarded,[7] from both the tradition of yesterday and the culture of today. Therefore, this framework looks for a creative incorporation of the triad of gospel, culture and modernity. In the light of this we will now look into various mission strategies:

5.2.1. Mission with the Youths

For the betterment of the youths, clear cut aims and objectives should be established for the Youth department. The individual youth needs to be encouraged to be committed to fulfilling Christian

---

[3] Can we be satisfied with the mission work that our churches are doing today? What kind of mission strategy will be effective for our present society?

[4] Interview with Deuhing..., Peren Town, 10 January 2009.

[5] Interview with Mirhu, President All Zeliangrong Student Union Assam Manipur and Nagaland, Dimapur, 11 January 2009. Hereafter Interview with Mirhu...

[6] *The Willowbank Report...*, 505.

[7] Practices like head hunting, drinking rice beer, and witchcraft or sorcery should be discarded.

identity and ministry.[8] Though youth constitutes one third of the total population, looking at the present trend of Christian mission and church ministry, the churches are not using the full potential of the youth.[9] The youth should be trained and brought up in a way that will make them conscious of their identity as Zeliangrong and Christian and become good citizens and responsible leaders; to reach this end the churches should work for and with the youth by creatively incorporating traditional culture, Christian principles and things of the contemporary world. But sadly ministry to and with the youths has been one sided and emphasized only on Christian values while neglecting the traditions and modernity for many years. The churches should change their approach to the youth and the pattern of youth ministry by incorporating the things which interest them from both the traditions and from the contemporary things, such as through the use of western musical instruments to give more room for the youth to participate in the life of the church worship in order to express their spiritual joy and freely worship.

The effective usage of sports ministry can help the youth to develop their strength both physically and spiritually. Most of the Zeliangrong youth like sports and some of them are very talented. The ZBCC Youth Department once conducted a tournament in

---

[8] Rev. R. Lalbiakliana, "Youth Ministry" *Compendium: The Baptist Church of Mizoram, in Honor of BMS Mission in Mizoram 1903-2003* (Serkawn: The Centenary Committee Baptist Church of Mizoram, 2003), 147. The Thalai Kristian Pawl (TKP) of BCM aims and objectives were; to help the youths to become good Christians, to train the youths to work for Christ and the church, to encourage and guide the youths to be useful for the society, and to help participate in the extension of God's Kingdom. And the TKP's ministry pledge *For Christ and the Church* states, "with full faith in my strength, Jesus Christ, I shall have fellowship with God every day. I shall always participate in our church worship services and all its activities. I shall work for the welfare of the society and for the strengthening of its unity, and I shall earnestly try to bring others to Christ."

[9] How effective are our mission activities towards the young people in our society? To this 75% of respondents answered that they are not satisfied with the way the churches are doing mission for and with the youths. Mr. D. Anui, Youth Secretary of ZBCC said that, "Young people are the victim to carry all the blame, and less concerns are towards them." Another Respondent said that the young people are most neglected in the mission.

October 2006 at *Jalukie* Town Baptist Church and found it to be fruitful.[10] Churches should give more emphasis and conduct a well-planned regular 'church sports week' every year which will include cultural games like wrestling, long jump, shot put, spear throwing and stone lifting,[11] to let the youth glorify God by making use of their talents and draw closer to the Lord. In addition to this, youth rallies, camps, seminars and symposiums may be conducted[12] in which the cultural values and traditional heritages can be imparted along with the teaching of the gospel in the contemporary world. For instance, in the traditional society the winner does not get any prize, but rather he has to give away his shawl *Pai* to an old man held in respect by the village. In return, by witnessing the game the old man would bless the athlete.[13] These good practices should be imparted to our youths today so as to incorporate the good things in our life.

5.2.2. Mission and Women

The church as the kingdom community is a place where everybody should get equal treatment and be content with oneself being a part of the community, and to do this the churches should be mindful to respect one another as co-partners. It is illogical to be biased on the basis of gender. Both men and women should actively participate in God's mission. However, the women have not been given equal

---

[10] The writer personally attended the said tournament and witnessed many youths who are not regular in church activities actively participating in the tournament. Football was played by the men and volleyball was played by the women; there was a special time of devotion every morning and evening worship service with many resourceful preachers who spoke to the youths in the tournament. Besides, the other Churches in the circle (Ngwalwa Area) also conducted Church Games and Sports meets and reported them to be satisfactory and successful, because many youths were drawn to the church related activities.

[11] Joseph Athickal, *Maram Nagas: A Socio-Cultural Study* (New Delhi: Mittal Publications, 1992), 100.

[12] Champhang Jajo, *Christian Life in a Tribal Context: in Manipur* (Calcutta: C. Jajo, 1990), 75-76.

[13] Joseph Athickal, *Maram Nagas...*, 100. The Zeliangrong tribes do the same when a person catches a mithun in the community chase. The oldest man among the group in the chasing party would remove the shawl of the person who caught the mithun, and in return bless the young man to be more successful in life.

privilege in the church and society on the grounds that they are women. For example, they have been expected to be a good mother, faithful wife and helper, but not expected to work as an ordained minister or as a pastor in the church.

The Synthesis of the three, contemporary context, gospel and culture should enhance mission work because in today's contemporary context women prove themselves to be the equals of men in every arena of life. There is a need for sound Biblical and doctrinal practices where both men and women work together as partners in God's mission,[14] since God also has given numerous gifts to women and they need to use them.[15] This would also relate to some relevant traditional cultural practices, because women in the traditional society also performed certain rites and religious duties as a priest, for example the sowing of the first seed and harvesting of the first corn, and in leading the bride to her bridegroom's house. Therefore, it is proper that the church also frees itself from the age old concept about women which hinders them from effectively involving in mission work. As mission belongs to God, God's mission is for all and all should do God's mission.

5.2.3. Toward Comprehensive Salvation

Unlike the traditional society, the society today is under the grip of social injustice, corruption, exploitation, economic dependency, discrimination, factionalism, bribery, substance abuse, alcoholism and broken homes. In this context the gospel should be understood from a holistic perspective as a means for the healing of a broken

---

[14] R. L. Hnuni, "Issues of women in Ministry" *Good News for the North East India: A Theological Reader*, ed., Renthy Keitzar (Guwahati: CLC, 1995), 192. The protestant doctrine of ministry is the 'priesthood of all believers' and absence of women in ordained ministry and leadership is against this doctrine as well as biblical teaching.

[15] Sakhi M. Athyal, "Biblical Basis for the Role of women in Mission" *Mission & Missions: Essays in Honour of I. Ben Wati*, Jey J. Kanagaraj ed., (Pune: Union Biblical Seminary, 1998), 112. They are great prayer warriors and excellent counselors. Women sympathetically understand people's needs. They were endowed with virtues like the ability to nurture children with compassion; they are people oriented.

society.[16] Christians should mediate comprehensive salvation.[17] The church mediatory mandate consists of multiple facets that together constitute a single undividable whole.[18] The church in God's mission represents a resistance movement against every manifestation of fatalism and quietism. In this regards Bosch made it clear that:[19]

Those who know that God will one day wipe away all tears will not accept with resignation the tears of those who are oppressed now... Anyone who believes that the enemy of God and humans will be vanquished will already oppose him now in his machinations in family and society. For all of this has to do with salvation. Therefore, the church should prophetically confront these evils and oppressive structure of the society by being standing on the side of the poor, oppressed, and the victims of this unjust society.

5.2.4. Theologically Motivated Mission

In the traditional society, though there were priests for the community, everyone was also a priest in their own right for themselves, since there is no separation between religious and secular, spiritual and carnal. Even the Protestant doctrine approves of the priesthood of

---

[16] Asenla, R. Simon and Elungkiebe, "Gospel and Tribal Culture: Naga Perspective" *Good News for North East India: A Theological Reader,* ed., Renthy Keitzar (Guwahati: CLC, 1995), 167.

[17] David J. Bosch, Transforming Mission: Paradigm Shifts in Theology of Mission, (Maryknoll, New York: Orbis Books, 1996), 400. Hereafter, Bosch, Transforming... Salvation is as coherent, broad, and deep as the needs and exigencies of human existence. Therefore, comprehensive mission means being involved in the ongoing dialogue between God, who offers his salvation, and the world, which – enmeshed in all kinds of evil - craves that salvation.

[18] J. D. Gort, "Human Distress, Salvation and Mediation of Salvation" *Missiology: An Ecumenical Introduction; Text and Context of Global Christianity,* eds., F. J. Verstraelen, *et al.,* (Michigan: William B. Eerdmans Publishing Company, 1995), 209. This mediatory mandate calls for the ministry of proclamation; to be summoned to faith and repentance and to reconcile with God and fellow creatures, a ministry of Mercy; through extension of help and assistance to all, the bearers of the gospel of liberation can never ignore or forget the plight of the poor and the oppressed, and the ministry of justice; advance the liberation of the poor and the oppressed by doing everything about social, political and economic order that it is as just as possible, both at hand and far away.

[19] Bosch, *Transforming...*, 400.

every believer. Our theology of mission has to be determined by our culture and the scripture. Therefore, it is imperative for every Christian to live a Christ-like life. Not everyone can be a paid missionary, but everyone can be missional in one's own profession discharging one's duty faithfully for the service of human-kind and God.[20] This sense of Christian living is needed to be restored and strengthened today. A Christian is still a missionary in his/her daily life, which the non-official or unpaid missionary must know.[21] If all Zeliangrong Christians consciously live out in this manner and reveal the secret of Christ's grace to others then they can be called a missionary and they can have a better effect on the society.

Many of the Zeliangrong Christians today are second and third generation Christians, they are Christians simply because they are born a Christian. Therefore, many do not know what exactly it is to be a Christian and fail to live in the light of the Christian principle and way of life. Proclamation is an important aspect of Christian witness. However, witnessing with personal life and church life is equally important. It is the family that lays the foundation for a Christian life, and prayer should therefore be central to the life and witness of the family. A sound Christian basis in the family would ensure a mature Christian growth.[22] But the Zeliangrong Christians seem to be failing to impart these Christian principles to their young ones at home. Here, the integration of the traditional system of parenting the children by giving oral teachings of their traditions and culture, and the biblical way of bringing up a child, and also the contemporary way of bringing up children in strict discipline will be

---

[20] Rolland Allen, "The Unofficial Missionary" Perspectives on World Mission South Asia Versions (Bangalore: New Life Literature, 1998), 284. Hereafter Rolland, Unofficial Missionary.... The missionary work of the 'unofficial missionary' is not the same work which a paid professional missionary does. The paid professional missionaries leave the ordinary work of the world and devote themselves to what they calls 'religious work' while the non professional missionary realizes that the ordinary work of the world ought to be done religiously, and does it religiously and calls it 'religious work'.

[21] Rolland, *Unofficial Missionary...*, 285.

[22] Jesudas M. Athyal, *Relevant Patterns of Christian Witness in India: People as Agents of Mission; Mission – Evangelism-Vol. I* (Thiruvalla: Christhava Sahithya Samity, 2000), 206.

helpful. Better Sunday school is also needed, which would provide the young Zeliangrong Christians with better faith formation.

5.2.5. Chaplaincy Ministry

Many children and young people in this contemporary society go to towns and cosmopolitan cities for better education and job opportunities, and as such the church could not extend her ministry and provide spiritual guidance and edification to the youngsters. In this context the traditional system of village to village friendship and the modern system of operating work through networking system should be an effective example for the ZBCAs to have good networking among the pastors in the villages and the pastors in towns and cities where the students stay. Therefore, proper networking among the church leaders is encouraged. For instance, the pastors of local churches can make a provisional certificate for the students and people working outside so that they can be taken care of by the pastors in those places wherever they go.

Besides, there are many schools and a few colleges coming up within the district, wherein many children and young people are flocking in for education; these institutions are the replacement of traditional boys' and girls' dormitories from where they learnt about social, moral, culture and everything about life under heaven. The elders are now the chaplains who discipline the youngsters. But, even in these places there is no proper arrangement to cater to the spiritual needs of the students except in some mission schools. Scripture is hardly taught in the government schools and colleges, and the teaching on culture is practically absent. So the need of the hour is to introduce effective chaplaincy ministry in the schools and colleges who can impart good moral, religious and spiritual teachings to the students, and also to inculcate good culture to the children and youths in these places.

5.2.6. Restructuring the Structure

The Zeliangrong traditional society is a communitarian society, which works together as community and for the community.[23] The global community of the contemporary world emphasizes the oneness and the unity of the whole people in the world, and the scripture also talks a great deal of the unity of the "Body of Christ" (Rom 12:5, 9, 10). Even Christ prayed for the unity of his disciples and the church that they may all be one (John 17: 11b, 20-21). Mr. Mirhu also asserts that there is a great need for the churches to work for unity.[24] It is clear that the divided structure of the ZBCAs needs re-evaluation.

It is due to the fragmented structure that the Associations are weak and powerless to do mission work effectively. All the four ZBCAs are autonomous in themselves, and do not have any ground for working together. The local churches within the Associations are again autonomous in terms of finance and church administration. The associations are managing through arbitrary budgeting and tithing system.[25] In this structure the associations are economically poorer than some of the big local churches, since there is no uniformity in church growth; rather, the gap is widened between the rich and the poor churches. The rich churches have two or three theologically trained fulltime workers while the poor churches do not even have a trained pastor. The associations feel the need to do mission work in a wider circle but due to financial constraints they could not do much.

So there is an immediate need to restructure the existing structure which will be relevant for the churches to promote equal growth of the church in both physical and spiritual realms. The existing

[23] Some may argue that the traditional communitarian society was only within the village community, but my point of argument here is the members of those village communities are also the members of the wider organization, so if the communitarian system of working together fits well with the smaller group then it will certainly be better for the larger community.

[24] Interview with Mirhu..., Dimapur, 11th January 2009.

[25] The ZBCC churches gives 10% tithe of the Church total income to the Association, the LBA churches gives 15% the, RBA and the ZBA give a fixed budget to their associations.

structure may have many advantages yet it is highly recommended to devise a better and more relevant structure for the wholesome growth of the churches.

5.2.6.1. A Convention

It would be very appropriate to have a Zeliangrong Baptist Churches Convention which will provide a common platform for all the four different Associations to work in collaboration with each other.

5.2.6.2. Centralized Association

Centralization would be another effective system for all the associations, which will boost their material and spiritual needs, as in this structure every power will be concentrated in the association. This structure will also open an opportunity to both the poor and rich churches to work together in greater unity for God's mission.[26]

5.2.7. Fulltime Pastoral Ministry

The Zeliangrong churches from their inception have been making good use of the lay people as church administrators, church workers, pastors and deacons. They are persons who have good standing in the society, being respected by the society and are capable of doing the work. The work of evangelism has been done through some few 'short term missionary/evangelists,'[27] and many of them are not theologically trained but work as evangelists because of the burning zeal that they have for the spread of the gospel. They are to be commended for the hardship that they have endured to sustain the church traditions and nurturing the churches despite their limited theological knowledge.

---

[26] The churches in Mizoram (Presbyterian, Baptist and Evangelical Church of Maryland) have a centralized system of administration. The Assembly or the Synod controls every power and manages the churches. Thus, the churches are prospering, growing together and doing God's mission dynamically.

[27] J. Herbert Kane, *Winds of Change in the Christian Mission* (Chicago: Moody Press, 1973), 143. Hereafter cited as J. H. Kane, *Winds of Change...* Short term missionaries return home without even getting to know the people and the congregation well. The ZBCC has a tendency of sending short term missionary/ project evangelists on some occasions like after a Jubilee celebration.

However, in a fast changing contemporary society, the mission of the church need fulltime theologically trained pastors,[28] missionaries and other church workers to effectively address to the need of the days. And the concept of fulltime ministry is very much culturally appropriate because the Zeliangrong priests were also lifetime priests until their death. So also the contemporary Christians of various denominational traditions have fulltime or lifetime workers in Christian ministry. The century old practice of having part time evangelists touring and ministering to the churches can be phased out to usher in fulltime pastors in all the churches.

5.2.8. Indigenous-creative worship

Integration of Christian faith with local culture is a dynamic and creative process. Culture is dynamic and changes as new situations arise.[29] The incarnation of Jesus affirms, fulfils, challenges and transforms cultures. The church too should become embodied in culture. As such a community, the church is called to relate itself to any culture critically, creatively and redemptively.[30] The communication of the gospel can be more effective through culture, language, structures, art, music, dance, and other expressions.

Worship is an expression of the acknowledgement that God is the creator, an expression of sincere reverence, humble confession, earnest prayer, faith and jealous commitment in our relationship with God.[31] In worship, an individual opens up one's heart and mind to the creator God and pays homage to the Lord. Worship

---

[28] The Pastors in the Zeliangrong Baptist Churches are in the real sense not fulltime workers; the fact is that, after few years of service they can be removed from pastoral work and became just like the other members in the congregation (even a theologically trained person is not a fulltime pastor in this sense). Many churches have Pastors who work voluntarily without a proper salary and they also engage in some other professions.

[29] Joseph Mattam & Sebastian Kim, *Dimensions of Mission in India* (Bombay: St. Paul's Publication, 1995), 158.

[30] Bethel Krupa "Church, Gospel and Cultures: A Case Study from the Parakal Mission" *The Community we Seek Perspective on Mission*, ed., Jesudas M. Athyal (Thiruvalla: Christian Sahitya Samithi, 2003), 144.

[31] Presbyterian Church of India, *Manual of Worship* (Shillong: PCI, 2002), 1.

should be contextualized to meet the profound needs of the people. However, this is not seen in most of the churches today due to the heavy dependence on an old-fashioned style of Western traditional Christian worship which in practice does not have much effect on the hearts of the people.

Therefore, the rigid and static worship patterns which are obsolete should be set aside and creativity should be freshly instilled in the worship. To be authentic, the churches need to be rooted deeper in the local soil. Indigenization of Christian faith and inculturation of the liturgy and the practices of the churches are essential for the evolution of a contextual worship to create more interest and enthusiasm through the guidance of the Holy Spirit so that worship will be lively and people can truly worship the living God. One of the examples for this can be the incorporation of indigenous tunes with gospel lyrics and the use of traditional drums with western and modern musical instruments in Christian worship.

5.2.9. Eco-Care Mission

The mission of God is for the well-being of the whole earth. Therefore, it is essential for today's Churches to be eco-minded in her participation in God's mission. The traditional society had maintained the equilibrium of the fragile natural world but the present society has been continually exploiting the eco-system to meet the individual thirst for wealth and power in spite of the alarming threat of global warming and imminent destruction of the created world. The church should create mass awareness through seminars on ecological problems so as to safeguard the world. The content of the message of salvation should not negate the world and the creations and focus only on humankind as God's plan of salvation but should include the World of nature (John 3: 16). The primary goal of mission is conversion towards God, to fellow-beings and to the environment with a sense of love and stewardship. We are also commanded to love God and our neighbors and to be responsible stewards of the environment.[32]

[32] F. Hrangkhuma, "Mission in Context" *Mission & Missions: Essays in Honour of I. Ben Wati,* Jey J. Kanagaraj ed., (Pune: Union Biblical Seminary, 1998), 125.

5.2.10. Mission of Love and Justice

What was once the most egalitarian society has become excruciatingly and shamelessly non-egalitarian today; just a few people capture all political power and social legislation, the means of production of goods and services and the distribution of wealth without common sense and for common welfare.[33] There is no love and justice in the society, and sadly the churches are not strong enough in proclaiming against the injustice and discrimination prevailing under the oppressive structure of the society. God wanted human beings to love one another as they love themselves (Lev. 19:18) and loving one another is an integral part of loving God. Struggle for justice is another important aspect of Christian mission, in which we need to empower the powerless and identify ourselves as one of them. The eighth century prophets were vocal about justice, as Justice is rooted in God, the God of the poor.[34] Jesus himself identified with the powerless as revealed on the cross.[35] Jesus' mission was a mission of liberation, justice and love (Lk. 4:18). The role of the church in doing God's mission is to have relevant message to those who are last and least and to proclaim the good news of assurance and liberation. The Christians should work in solidarity with the poor and the oppressed and accept the reality of society in order to work together to rebuild it with the spirit of love and justice. It is theologically, culturally and contextually essential to love and work for justice.

5.2.11. Mission Constants in Context

Jesus effectively communicated the gospel of the Kingdom of God to various people according to their contexts. He did not change the

---

[33] Sebastian Karotemprel, "Mission and Evangelization in North East India: A Brief Theological Analysis" *Mission Today Subaltern Perspectives. Mission- Evangelism Studies, vol. II, ed.,* Jesudas M. Athyal, (Thiruvalla: Christava Sahitya Samithi, 2201), 94. Hereafter cited as Karotemprel, *Mission and Evangelization…*

[34] M. Mani Chacko, "Prophetic Insights for Contemporary Mission" *Mission Today: Challenges and Concerns* (Chennai: Mission, Ecumenism & Dialogue Department Gurukhul Lutheran Theological College, 1998), 165.

[35] K. C. Abraham, *Liberative Solidarity: Contemporary Perspective on Mission* (Thiruvalla: Christava Sahitya Samithi, 2001 2nd edition), 67.

content of the message but only the form of communication.[36] The churches are appearing to be pro-rich and pro-righteous, and the poor and the unrighteous are ignored and neglected.[37] The churches should attempt to carry out a ministry or mission loyal to the gospel and relevant for all the people within the cultural context.

5.2.12. Unity/Collaboration in Mission; Mission in Unity

In the Christian world the 20th century has been a century of ecumenism. Ecumenism is a new search for wholeness and unity and for overcoming dualism and dividedness. Ecumenical cooperation between churches have been taking place since the 1920s.[38] The Zeliangrong churches should also cross the boundaries of denominational churches, ignore their differences and join hands as

---

[36] S. D. Ponraj, *Missionary Anthropology: An Introduction* (Chennai: Mission Educational Books, 2004), 64, 65. His approach to the Jewish religious leader was in the form of dialogue which is more reasoning and logical, 'You must be born again'. To the Samaritan women his plea was simple and related to her daily needs of water and led her to understand her needs for the living water. To the fishermen, he invited them to become fishers of men, to the farmers he talked about soil, sowing seed, and harvesting, and they understood and responded to him.

[37] While I was working in a local church two years ago, I personally heard many people saying that the churches do not give attention to the poor and the needy, but rather that the church is like a fashion parade where the rich demonstrate their wealth. The community gathered in the church frown at drunkards with dislike. It is no longer accommodating but segregating the congregation in terms of wealth, strength and education.

[38] See O. L. Snaitang, "Christianity and social Transformation in North East India" Missiology for the 21st Century: South Asian Perspective, eds., Roger E. Hedlund & Paul Joshua Bhakiaraj (Delhi: ISPCK/MIIS, 2004), 393: In India the churches have joined together to form one united church like the CSI in 1947 and CNI in 1970, but the development of this trend in NEI has been somewhat discouraging. Bosch, Transforming Mission..., 464, 465. The national "council of churches" that was formed can only make sense if they serve the missio Dei. Ecumenism is not a passive and semi-reluctant coming together but an active and deliberate living and working together. Mission in unity is from the gifts of God the one Body of Christ. God's people are one; Christ's Body is one. Ecumenism is possible where people accept each other despite differences. The goal of ecumenism is not a fellowship exempt from conflict, but one which is characterized by unity in reconciled diversity.

partners in the mission of God, to work and live out the Kingdom values in love and unity for greater and effective mission.

5.2.13. Giving Ministry

The ministry of Christian giving is born from the greatest gift ever given to humankind, the gift of God in the person of Jesus Christ who is the only son of God. None, who had received Jesus Christ, could ever withhold the Good news; every true Christian feels compelled to share the Good news to others.[39] Giving is the nature of God and the children of God should also be willing to give. Traditionally, Zeliangrong people are generous in giving and sharing, even the rich stored their wealth to feed the community. It is also biblically sound to be generous (II Cor. 9: 7b, Acts 20: 35). However, the Zeliangrong churches today are not very cheerful in giving.[40] Therefore, they need to make a giant leap in this area.

5.2.14. Friendly mission to religious neighbours

Living in a religiously pluralistic world, the Zeliangrong Christians are not exempted from the challenges of religious pluralism in her endeavor in mission. With this backdrop our approach in mission to people of other faiths should be friendly, approachable and respectful, willing to listen to their story and also faithfully and sincerely witnessing Christ by telling our own story. Even traditionally, in spite of their headhunting culture, Zeliangrong people are friendly, neighborly and hospitable to others; this quality is also prescribed in the Scripture (Luke 10:25-37 - the parable of the Good Samaritan).

5.2.15. Spirit filled Mission

In God's mission we see that the triune God, God the Father, God the Son and God the Holy Spirit were actively involved. In the mission of Jesus we see God the Father (Mathew 3:17, John 10: 30 &38) and God the Holy Spirit (Luke 4: 18) were actively involved

---

[39] Rev. T. C. Laltlawmlova, "Giving Ministry in the Baptist Church of Mizoram" *Compendium: The Baptist Church of Mizoram, in Honor of BMS Mission in Mizoram, 1903-2003* (Serkawn: The Centenary Committee Baptist Church of Mizoram, 2003), 120.

[40] Interview with Kuzierang..., Peren Town, 9 October 2008.

and in the mission of the disciples we see the active involvement of God the Spirit by endowing the gift of Holy Spirit (Acts 2:1-4) who empowered them. In our mission today, alongside our creative and innovative mission strategies we need the empowerment of the Holy Spirit to guide and sustain us and to convict the people of their sins and helplessness. The World Council of Churches at its seventh assembly, Canberra 1991, devoted herself to the Theology and work of the Holy Spirit in the church, calling the church to mission and unity. The Spirit-filled mission is mission in Christ's way, through preaching, teaching and healing.[41]

5.3. Indigenous Zeliangrong Christian Identity

The nature of the Indigenous Zeliangrong Christian Identity in the light of our above discussion would be that of a society in which much emphasis is given to both community solidarity and expression of individual identity based on fusion of both tradition and modernity. There will be partnership of women and men in the mission and ministry of the Zeliangrong churches by means of doing away with the mindset of the patriarchal society. There will also be a creative fusion of indigenous tunes fused with modern music and use for worship, dance and celebration in the worship life and in the society. It will also be a society where both the poor and the rich will live together in peace and harmony, fulfilling the needs of one another.

Conclusion

The above discussions are some of the mission activities proposed towards a meaningful indigenous Zeliangrong Christianity and for a relevant contextual mission. The mission of the churches in her participation in God's mission should address the entire needs of the people and the created world. To reach this end, the whole members of the churches should involve in mission by being faithful to the Scripture and relevant to the cultural context of the people. Ultimately, it should work for the redemption of the whole humankind and the world.

---

[41] James A. Scherer and Stephen B. Bevans, eds., New Directions in Mission and Evangelization 1 (Maryknoll, New York: Orbis Books, 1998), 84, 87.

CONCLUSION

The end of this work calls for starting a more effective and dynamic mission which the Zeliangrong churches can carry out and accomplish. It is also the beginning of a call to all the Zeliangrong Christian leaders and all individual Christians to join in the endeavor and work effectively to bring it to its fulfillment.

The study has introduced the Zeliangrong people and discussed about their origin and migration, socio-cultural-political and religious life and showed that they share a common origin having common ancestors, common affinity and common cultural heritage and experiences. The Zeliangrong on the whole trace their origin to *Makuilongdi* village from where they dispersed to their present habitats. They were religiously devoted, economically self-sufficient, politically independent and socially communitarian, guided by the principle of *leirau* in which everyone had their role to play for the welfare of the community.

Chapter two discussed the advent of Christianity to the Zeliangrong people in the last part of the 19th century, with Mr. Heizieluing of Benreu village being the first Zeliangrong to embrace Christianity in 1897. Christianity was not welcomed by the people and the early converts were persecuted by their kinsmen but the church survived the hard times and made a rapid growth and thus, the formation of the Zeliangrong Baptist Associations took place. When the Kohima Mission Field held its Annual Association at Chalkot from March 20-22, 1926 the Joint Association of Zeliang and Kuki Christians was inaugurated and was called Zeliang-Kuki

Baptist Association, followed by the formation of the Zeliang Baptist Association which was later changed to the Zeliangrong Baptist Association and finally many other Zeliangrong Baptist Associations. Initially, Christianity brought the people together but as time passed, different associations and denominations divided them into many groups.

The encounter and interaction of the Zeliangrong culture and Gospel is extremely fascinating. The third and fourth chapters have shown that the Zeliangrong people were not very enthusiastic about responding to and accepting the gospel. However, in God's own work through the impact of the Revival awakening over Nagaland, the Zeliangrong people had accepted the Gospel and Christian faith. But, initially there was a strong resistance to Christianity, looking at it as a foreign religion by the traditional religious people and the *Heraka* reform cult. At the beginning the growth of Christianity was slow and pathetic, as many of the early converts were deliberately persecuted and even ostracized from their villages. As a result, the early converts had initially disliked the culture and traditions; the missionaries also partly failed on their part because they had a negative attitude towards the culture of the people.

The history of the Zeliangrong churches can be divided into two different periods, viz., 1897-1953, during which the churches were under the care of the *Kohima* Mission Field, and the second period from 1953 till date. The influence of modernity that has been brought about by the education imparted by the missionaries and the new system of government introduced by the British government strongly influenced their society leading to confusion of identity. There were not many attempts for indigenization of Christianity into the culture during the first period. However, this process has begun at a very slow pace in the second period when the churches became independent from other authorities. The efforts of indigenization have contributed to the forming of identity of the Zeliangrong Christians. The Revival awakening in the Zeliangrong area in 1970s contributed a lot to the development of the identity of the Zeliangrong Christians and the mission endeavor of the churches.

The identity of the Zeliangrong Christianity was more extraordinarily marked by the cultural continuity that they preserved in their lives; they could do so because Christianity was presented to the Zeliangrong in a context where indigenous religion was firmly founded. However, there lies a great task for the Zeliangrong Christians to creatively incorporate their good traditional heritages in their ecclesiastical worship life. As of now there is a great dividing line between social life and church life.

Finally, the fifth chapter was entitled, "Towards a meaningful indigenous Zeliangrong Christianity and a Relevant Contextual Mission". Here, the present state of the Zeliangrong Christians and the mission works of the associations in this dynamically changing world was discussed and the need to improve the situation of Zeliangrong Christians and their mission strategies was emphasized. This work was concluded by proposing various mission activities and strategies that would be contextually relevant in order to foster genuine and meaningful Indigenous Zeliangrong Christians, and for their effective mission. However, as time passes, we can expect further research for newer and more relevant mission strategies that will be suited for the dynamically changing culture.

Appendix–I

MISSION ACTIVITIES OF THE ZELIANGRONG BAPTIST CHURCH ASSOCIATIONS

Mission of the Zeliangrong Christians

With the acceptance of the gospel and their conversion to the Christian faith the Zeliangrong experienced love, joy, freedom and salvation through Christ. As a result they actively involved themselves in mission work. From the very initial stage of the church and during the formation of the Zeliang-Kuki Association the mission work was carried out mainly by the native people to her own citizens through the means of preaching. Then in the 1980's the Association was divided into various associations and each association has been doing the mission work in their own ways in various capacities. We shall look into the mission work of all the Associations in brief.

1. Mission activities Common to all the Associations

1.1. Evangelism

Evangelism is one of the common activities done by employing various means like preaching, teaching and sharing the gospel so that all may know the truth and come to Christ and live a Christ-like life.

1.2. Music

Music has been an integral part of mission and evangelism; the main purpose of music is to bring people to Christ, develop a lively worship service, and to nourish the spiritual life of the people. The contribution of music in Christian mission is as significant as preaching the word of God. Considering this, ZBCC is encouraging music ministry in the churches and organizing and producing cassettes. The Churches conduct music training and music camps, and also organize music festivals.

1.3. Philanthropic activities

One of the methods of doing mission by Zeliangrong churches is through philanthropic activities, since mission work includes attending to both the spiritual and physical needs of a person. Some of the areas in which they get involved are in helping the poor, extending help to the needy in different places, and to the victims of natural calamities, etc.[1] All these social services may not have direct evangelistic value but they are a part of preparation for evangelism.

1.4. Literature

Literature is a must for proclaiming the gospel to the people, so one of the biggest projects of the Zeliangrong churches is Bible translation. All the four Associations have a Bible and hymn book in their own local dialect. The Zeliangrong churches also gave importance to literature works and so gradual development is seen in the field of literature. Important journals like *Samlia* and *Chailihei* are published regularly.[2] For greater mission, the churches encourage people to write and translate books and articles which can be useful in sharing the gospel.

[1] Interview with Hiakie, field Evangelist and Former Mission Secretary, ZBCC, Mission Centre, Peren, on 1st November, 2008.

[2] *Samlia* is the Zeme Baptist Church council's Bulletin, and *Cailihei* is a theological journal.

1.5. Gospel Camps and crusades

Gospel camps and crusades are another important tool for evangelism, being used by the Zeliangrong evangelists, missionaries, and churches in their mission endeavors. This incurs heavy expenses but it proves helpful in renewing people's spiritual life, sharing the gospel and winning more souls.[3]

1.6. Church planting

Church planting is another feature common to all the Zeliangrong churches. Wherever the missionaries or evangelists go, conversion takes place and new converts are organized into a fellowship and then a local church. From the very beginning, the early Zeliangrong Christians were active in converting and planting churches.

1.7. Educational Mission

The educational mission of the ZBCAs is introduced to impart secular and religious education.[4] J. Herbert Kane has rightly pointed out that "Education has always been an integral part of the missionary movement…teaching held an important place in the public ministry of Christ."[5] Three of the four Zeliangrong Associations have established Schools being managed by the

---

[3] *ZBCC Samlia Vol- 5…* 14, 15. Gaili Baptist Church pastor reports of a Gospel Camp conducted in his church on 11th – 13th July 2008. He stated that 5person took water baptism, 24 persons were restored back to the church and 89 persons rededicated themselves for the service of the Lord. Mr. Diteibui the Church Secretary of New Puilo Baptist Church also reported the grant success of the Home Crusade program.

[4] The Mission schools do not only impart secular education but it is also meant for evangelism. Devotions are held every morning before classes and biblical truths are instructed to the students.

[5] J. Herbert Kane, *Understanding Christian Mission* (Grand Rapids, Michigan: Baker Book House, 1974), 318.

associations. Viz., LBA,[6] ZBA[7] and ZBCC.[8] In addition to this the ZBCC churches are also helping the Mission English School in Bendramai (Ze) by supporting mission teachers.[9] The motive for sending missionary teachers is to engage in evangelism through home visitation, camping and preaching along with their teaching assignment.[10]

---

[6] Interview with Kamwang Rentta, ES, LBA, an ordained minister, Tening, 16 October 2009, hereafter Interview with Kamwang...The Liangmai Baptist Association is running a Baptist High School at their mission headquarter, Tening Town. The School is attached with a residential hostel; it has classes from Nursery to 10th standard with 335 students and 17 staff members taking care of the educational affairs. According to the LBA budget of 2007, the LBA has sanctioned Rs. 50,000 towards the mission school out of her total budget of Rs. 6, 94, 820.

[7] Interview with *D. Kupwa...*,9 October 2008. The ZBA is also running two mission schools to impart education and moral guidance to the children with Christian principles. It has two mission Schools, one at Nsong known by name Eden English School; it has classes from Nursery to class 6, with 180 students. The other at Nkeo 'B' is known by the name Green Valley School, from Nursery to class 5, with 170 students being sponsored and run by the Khonoma Baptist Church through the Angami Baptist Church Council.

[8] See Souvenir, *ZBAN...*, 22-23; Ramdeu Nsa, "A historical study of the Zeme Baptist Church Council (Nagaland)" (B.D. thesis, Eastern Theological college, 2003), 49. The ZBCC has established three mission schools viz., "Baptist English School, Peren" in 1964, and Baptist School, Samjiuram in 1970 and finally Baptist English School, Ngwalwa in 1980. Now these schools were all upgraded to class 10 standard, however since recently the ZBCC is running only the Baptist High School Peren. The other two Schools at Jalukie and Ngwalwa were given to Mrs. Nini Meru and Mr. Mongzeung Mpom to manage on a contract basis by paying tax to the ZBCC, as the schools could not manage themselves.

[9] The Mission English School was established by the Jotsoma Baptist Church in the early 1980's and now this School has been handed over to the churches in that circle. Jostoma Baptist Church is a member church of Angami Baptist Church Council. The ZBCC is privileged to extend her helping hand to this Mission School by supporting the teachers who are working as missionary teachers.

[10] Hiakie Hegui, Mission Secretary, Report at ZBCC 57th Annual Session, Zeme Baptist Church Dimapur, 18-20 January 2008. Hereafter, Hiakie Hegui, *Mission Secretary, Report ...*

2. Mission Activities of Different Associations

2.1. Mission of the Liangmai Baptist Aruang

The Constitution of the Liangmai Baptist Aruang's Article III contains the Aims and Objectives of the Association. According to their constitution, the LBA engages in the mission works as discussed below.[11]

2.1.1. Home Mission

The LBA also not only give attention to the field of education and outside mission but it gives equal importance to home mission by sending project evangelists. A project evangelist works particularly among the six Liangmai villages out of the 17 churches.[12] In addition to this there are also other churches which have their own evangelists working among them. For example, New Jalukie (LBC) has two evangelists at present.[13] The LBA in collaboration with the Nagaland Baptist Church Council, the state education department and the Central government participates in the SSA program and runs alternative schooling in eight villages in their jurisdiction. This mission enables the church to reach the young high school drop-outs with better care and caters to their need as not all the young people have the privilege to go to school.

2.1.2. Outreach Mission

The LBA is also sending Mr. Baule Wangnao as a missionary to Hangya Mission area to the eastern Naga people living in Myanmar.[14] They raised funds to sponsor the missionary through each household

---

[11] Constitution of the Liangmai Baptist Association, p. 2, states the following 1) Promote missionary enterprise; develop human resources, society and economy. 2) Make the love of God manifest through the humanitarian and social services and development programs. 3) Establish institutions, enterprise, training centres and other humanitarian services. 4) Seek and apply for funds from Christian agencies or government or funding organizations both from within and without the country.

[12] Interview, *Kamwang...*

[13] Tunchapbo, A theological Student from LBA, Aizawl theological College, 27 January 2009. The two evangelists are Mr. Asuibo and Mr. Aduanbo.

[14] Rev. Kamwang Rentta, LBA Executive Secretary Report at NBCC 71st Annual Session at Kiusor, February, 1-3, 2008. Hereafter Kamwang, ES Report...

donating a cock. The LBA also supervises the local churches to send missionaries. As such, Tening Village Church sent two missionaries, one to Indo-Bhutan and another to Halflong, North Cachar district of Assam.[15] At present LBA is supporting 7 evangelists working in Jammu and Kashmir and 8 evangelists working in the Assam Tinsukia area.[16]

2.2. Mission of RBA

The RBA, by standing firm to her motto, *Spread God's Love* and her theme, *Press on to the Goal* envisages the extension of God's Kingdom through evangelistic and philanthropic works, in order to promote peace and wholesomeness here on earth. The RBA is profoundly committed to follow the wholesome ministry of our Lord Jesus by maintaining the balance between the spiritual and physical needs of the constituent member churches, the members of different denominations and those of other faiths.[17]

2.2.1. Spiritual development

They give first preference to spiritual development programs for spiritual and moral nurturing. They undertake programs like training, seminars, Bible studies and camps for various age groups. They have also sent 11 missionaries to Assam and Arunachal Pradesh.[18]

---

[15] Interview, *Kamwang*...

[16] Kitanwi, ES, LBA, telephone interview, 4 April 2018.

[17] *20th Foundation RBA*.... The Rongmei Baptist Association in Nagaland has been participating in the mission of God, functioning its ministry in two ways, viz., nurturing the spiritual and temporal or physical well being of the individuals. *First,* Spiritual ministry is given priority as it is most essential for personal salvation and growth of every person professing the Christian faith. The Association has been administering these requirements to the local churches through the general administration of the association. *Secondly,* Charitable work is the other side of her ministry. Looking at the present scenario of the rapid rise of poverty and landlessness in the region, the Association committed herself to uplift the people who are in the lowest ebb in their spiritual and socio-economic status through developmental activities.

[18] Mathiuthai, Executive Secretary, RBA, telephone interview, 5 April 2018.

2.2.2. Developmental works

The Association has taken up a project called Peoples Integrated Development Services (PIDS)[19] mainly for organising philanthropic activities for the whole people in the region. The association in this endeavor has been working in co-operation with various governmental departments and various people. Through PIDS, the RBA has been doing the following activities:

2.2.2.1. Economic development

The Christians as individuals and as a corporate group need finance for the mission work and also for self-sustaining. Therefore, they give equal importance to the economic development of the people. For this, the RBA involves in income-generating programs for women's groups, farmers, drop out youths and the landless.

2.2.2.2. Community development

The RBA have stepped beyond just religious activities since 1992 by envisaging holistic mission and giving importance to community development for the physical welfare of the community. For this end they undertake programs like water resource programs, health and sanitation, and construction of community halls. The RBA also diligently conducts workshops for giving awareness about environmental problems and conflict management, gives training on development and accountancy, helps in forming women SHG groups and helps them by partnering with the National Bank for Agriculture and Rural Development (NABARD). They provide career guidance to the youth and also Agriculture and Horticulture

---

[19] "Peoples Integrated Development Services" A Pamphlet of the RBA., nd. PIDS believes in strong collaboration with the people to undertake development that is integral, regarding gender, culture and customs, education and environmental sensitivity to sustain socio-economic conditions and people's well-being with active participation so that the people take the responsibility for their destiny. It aims at socio-economic upliftment of the marginalized rural poor, motivating and promoting education, revitalizing and keeping good customary practices relevant for today, to emancipate the people to know their rights through conscientizing, to create gender equality and equity, to take up eco-friendly programs and to develop networking with various Non-Governmental organizations and the government.

training to the farmers. Vocational skill development programs are also taken up to support the craftsmen and carpenters. It also helps the students in the field of education by providing tuition fees, note books and other kits for school going children. The RBA has been extending these programs to the constituent church members and to the neighboring villages. The Association's activities spread across 40 villages among 2000 families in the Peren district of Nagaland. Their mission has been very successful in translating the gospel into the people's context as they integrate faith and economic development.[20]

2.3. Mission of the ZBA

The ZBA in her participation in God's mission have four ordained ministers, three evangelists and one full time trained pastor.[21] The ZBA is carrying out her mission in partnership with the Ao Baptist Arogo Mungdang (ABAM).[22]

2.3.1. Home Mission

Under the Home Mission, the Zeme Baptist Association (ZBA) has been doing the work of evangelism through the Nehemiah Mission to the *Heraka* people in their region. They have Mr. Deisam Pame as their evangelist being sponsored by Nehemiah India.[23] At present ZBA has four evangelists working within their jurisdiction.[24]

---

[20] Ajit Kanitkar, *How Church group helped better the lot of Tribal villagers in Nagaland's Jalukie Valley.* https://scroll.in, accessed on 3/4/2018 Aizawl.

[21] Rev. Bikau Pame, Rev. B. Haisong, Rev. Dr. Rabi Pame and Rev Teubui kome.

[22] Interview with Cilak Pame, President Zeme Theological Association North East India, Jalukie Town, 4 January 2009. Hereafter, Interview, *Cilak Pame…*, 4 January 2009. ABAM has sponsored two staff salaries from 1989-2007 viz., their Executive secretary and Rev. Namtiubui's salary. At present the ABAM has been sending Mr. R. Tally as a missionary working among the people.

[23] Interview, Cilak Pame…, 4 January 2009. R. Tally is being sponsored by three Ao churches of Peren Town, Jalukie Town and Sugar Mill.

[24] Teubei, Former ES, ZBA, telephone interview, 3 April 2018.

2.3.2. Outreach Mission

The ZBA, not content with just the Home mission has taken up the outreach mission work from 2008 and has selected the Kebai area of NC Hills Assam to work among the Kacharis. They have been sending an evangelist, Mr. Namwang Neume, to the Kacharis.[25]

2.4. Mission of the ZBCC

The Constitution of the ZBCC states that the ZBCC churches which had a common tribal origin has established a group with a plan to accomplish what is assigned to the believers; this constitution was carefully prepared and a declaration was made on 24th January 1982. Secondly, the ZBCC churches in unity are committed to do the work of the Kingdom of God within and outside the ZBCC area. To engage in developmental works and philanthropic activities for the Kingdom of God, the ZBCC is committed to work in collaboration with other groups and organizations.[26]

For wider and effective participation in God's mission, ZBCC formed the Mission Department on 16th Nov, 1988.[27] Today, the Mission Department is one of the most important departments under ZBCC. In 2008, Mr. Hiapierai was the Mission Secretary with five other members. At present there are thirty persons working as evangelists and missionaries.[28] The Mission department is affiliated to the NMM and is working with different mission agencies. The mission department's income in 2008 was Rs. 9,08,174/- and the proposed budget for 2009 was Rs. 13,97,696.[29]

---

[25] Interview, *Cilak Pame...*, 4 January 2009.

[26] Constitution of the Zeliangrong Baptist Church Council, 24th January 1982.

[27] "Mission Department ZBCC Ha" ZBCC Samlia vol.6, (September, 2008): 14. Hereafter, ZBCC Samlia Vol. 6.... The Executive Secretary was the caretaker of the department for the first ten years. However, the full-fledged mission department was formed in 1998 with Mr. Hiakie Hegui as the first Mission Secretaryfor better functioning of the department.

[28] *ZBCC Samlia Vol. 6...*, 14. The other five members 1) Mr. Atippe Mhainamtsi, 2) Mr. Kwetranglu Azailong, 3) Mr. Ilwa Kezanglwa, 4) Mr. Bamdi Peren, 5) Mr. Leusi, Ngwalwa.

[29] Interview with Hiapierai, Mission Secretary ZBCC, Peren Town, 29th January 2009.

The budget of the mission department for the current year is Rs. 46,49,175 and Mr. Ramdeu Nsa is the present Mission Secretary of the council.[30]

2.4.1. Functions of Mission Department

The Mission Department functions as the arm of the Council pertaining to missions and plays a vital role. The Mission Department functions with the contributions of the individuals on Mission Day of the ZBCC churches, and with a certain amount set apart as the budget for mission work by the Council.[31] There is no clear statement given for the functions and visions of Mission Department. However, their write ups in *ZBCC Samlia Vol. 6…,* 14, 15, highlights their positions; viz., (1) To mobilize, exhort and encourage the churches to proclaim the gospel in collaboration with other Christians. (2) To generate funds, train the missionaries and assist missionaries and evangelists, so as to effectively witness to the whole world. (3) To provide material needs to the needy (nurturing the sick, educating and improving the living standards) and (4) To supervise all the Mission works of the churches through the guidance and vision of the Council, and to carry out the resolutions and plans of the committee.[32] The ZBCC in relation to these points engages in mission work; the same can be classified into two categories, viz., Home Mission and Outreach Mission.

2.4.2. Home Mission

2.4.2.1. Medical

God's goal in mission is to bring about the Messianic kingdom. The kingdom addresses every need of a person, such as the spiritual, moral, material, physical, social, cultural and political needs.[33] One of the important mission activities of the ZBCC is the medical

[30] Mr. Izieteilung, Executive Secretary ZBCC, telephone interview, 9 April 2018.

[31] Hiakie Hegui, *Mission Secretary, Report …*

[32] *ZBCC Samlia Vol. 6…,* 14-15.

[33] J.Verkuyl, *Contemporary Missiology: An Introduction* (William B. Eerdmans, 1987), 211.

mission. It helps the people by distributing free medicine to the sick. It also sells medicine to the people at a cheaper rate.[34] The aim of physical healing or medical healing is of longevity, and the biblical understanding of healing and spiritual healing would aim at fullness of life or eternal life.[35] The ZBCC also feels that physical and mental healing is the very essence of the gospel of the grace of God. As Jesus' ministry also includes a healing dimension (Mathew 10:8), the ZBCC started a medical mission for physical healing and this is very much relevant in the present society.

2.4.2.2. Vernacular Bible School

Another important activity is giving training to the local church leaders in the Vernacular Bible School. This is conducted annually for a month or two. The motive for forming this training is to give intensive study on the Bible so that they will be able to help their congregation in their own local churches. This school is mainly for the lay people.

2.4.2.3. Prayer House and Healing Centers

The healing centre is another important mission strategy undertaken by the Council. The council feels that mission is not confined to preaching alone. Therefore, with a wider vision in doing mission, two important prayer/healing centers were established at *Jalukie* town and *Ngwalwa* recently. The main activities in these centers were prayer and fasting, and herbal medicines are given when necessary. Many are blessed through this ministry.[36]

---

[34] *ZBCC Samlia Vol. 6…*, 15.

[35] George Isaac, "Mission and Healing", *Mission Paradigm in the New Millennium*, W.S. Milton Jeganathan, ed., (Delhi: ISPCK, 2001), 357-378.

[36] Pauhia, "ZBCC Kekie ki ha mdu kegai" *ZBCC Samlia, Vol. 5* (August 2008): 7, 8. The prayer house in charge has reported for the months of March – May and said that 281 persons have visited the ZBCC Prayer house for healing and spiritual renewal.

2.4.3. Outreach Mission

2.4.3.1. Mission in N. C. Hills, Assam

With their deep commitment for God's mission and concern for the people, the ZBCC has been sending missionaries to N.C. Hills, Assam as one of their Mission Fields. They have been sponsoring evangelists, missionaries, teachers, Women Secretary and Executive Secretary of the ZBAA.[37] The motive of ZBCC in doing mission in N.C. Hills is to save individual souls by proclaiming the gospel of Jesus Christ. Through the active mission of the missionaries and the natives, today many of them are embracing the Christian faith.

2.4.3.2. Mission in Myanmar

In partnership with the Council of Naga Baptist Churches (CNBC) the ZBCC has been supporting seven missionaries who are working in the Somra Area of Myanmar. The same area has been taken as the ZBCC mission field with a plan to intensify the work there.[38]

2.4.3.3. Mission in Uttar Pradesh (UP) and Nepal

To widen the vision of their mission, the ZBCC also sent a missionary teacher to the Oriental English School-Nautanwa (UP), and another teacher to work at Chetriri village in Nepal through the supervision of the United Himalayan Mission (UHM). These mission teachers teach the students and also do the work of evangelism through visiting non-Christian homes and conducting prayer fellowship

---

[37] Mission Department, ZBCC, "Missionaries, Evangelists nah Kepeimeze Nqwa, kelak nah nli ne ngha eh heta tei kebam" nd.The Zeliangrong people live in three states mainly in Manipur, Nagaland and Assam. Almost 40% of the Zeme live in N. C. hills and here 80% of the people are non-Christians. They follow the 'traditional religion' and Heraka which is still very strong among the Zeme people in Assam. The following persons are reported to be working in N. C. Hills 1) Mr. Kailiwangbou 2) Mr. Bamdi 3) Mr. Namzie 4) Mr. Asuibo 5) Mr. Keheubuing 6) Mr. Deisungbe 7) Mr. Bamrai 8) Mr. Amangbe 9) Ms. Ameile Riame 10) Mr. Rangumsing 11) Alile.

[38] Interviewed Mr. Hiapierai, Mission Secretary ZBCC, Peren Town, 28th January, 2009.

with the believers. The mission teachers are sponsored by the local churches back at home.[39]

2.4.3.4. Additional mission activities at present

Currently the ZBCC Mission Department sends four home evangelists to work among the Heraka people, one home evangelist to the Jalukie valleys and one project evangelist to the non-locals living in the jurisdiction of ZBCC. The Department also sends out 6 missionaries to the Olo tribe in Tirap district of Arunachal, 1 to Karbianglong, 3 to Nepal and 2 to Odisa.[40]

---

[39] *ZBCC Samlia Vol. 6…*, 3-4.

[40] Mr. Ramdeu Nsa, Mission Secretry, ZBCC, telephone interview, 9 April 2018.

Appendix–II

QUESTIONNAIRE

Respondent's Particulars

Name :

Sex :

Designation :

Address :

Tick the appropriate one

1. All the ZLRs cultural practices and way of life are good.
   Yes [ ] No [ ] Don't know [ ]
   Any comment:

2. We have to select and use only the liberative cultural elements for today.
   Yes [ ] No [ ] Don't know [ ]

3. Christian religion is better than traditional culture and it does not need traditional culture.
   Yes [ ] No [ ] Don't know [ ]
   Reason why Yes or No:

4. The ZLR Christians should use traditional tunes and dances in praising and worshipping God.
   Yes [ ]   No [ ]   Don't know [ ]

5. In the truest sense, can we say that our foreparents are really religious people in their life?
   Yes [ ]   No [ ]   Don't know [ ]

6. Are the present ZLR peoples devoted in our Christian living like our fore parents?
   Yes [ ]   No [ ]   Don't know [ ]

7. Has the encounter between Christianity and ZLR culture affected only the
   ZLR Christians [ ] ZLR Non-Christians [ ] Both the groups [ ]
   Any comment:

8. Will the ZLR Christians' participation in the Mission of God be successful without being relevant to the culture and present life situation of the people?
   Yes [ ]   No [ ]   Don't know [ ]

9. Who are they that profess Christianity in our society? What is their identity?
   Zeliangrong [ ]   Christians [ ]   Zeliangrong Christians [ ]

10. Can we really blame Christianity for the deterioration of our culture today?
   Yes [ ]   No [ ]   Don't know [ ]
   Any comment? [

Please kindly answer in few sentences

1. How do you perceive today's culture of our society?

2. Is there the combination of cultural elements and Christian elements in the life of the ZLR Christians?

3. As a Christian minister/ pastor/ theological trained person/ church leader, are you contented with the nature of our present society?

4. To what extent the ZLR Christian have included the cultural elements in their life.

5. Will it be better if we accommodate more of ZLR culture in our Christian living?

6. Can we be satisfied with the mission work that our churches are doing today?

7. How effective are our mission activities towards the young people in our society?

8. What kind of mission strategy will be effective for our present society?

9. To what extent has the Christian faith transformed the ZLR society?

BIBLIOGRAPHY

Books

Abraham, K. C. *Liberative Solidarity: Contemporary Perspective on Mission.* Thiruvalla: Christava Sahitya Samithi, 2001 2nd edition.

Aleaz, K. P. *The Gospel of Indian Culture.* Calcutta: Punthi Pustak, 1994.

Allen, B. C, *et al.* eds. *Gazetter of Bengal and the North East India.* Delhi: Mittal Publications, 1976.

Aosenba. *The Naga Resistance Movement: Prospect of Peace and Armed Conflict.* New Delhi: Regency Publications, 2001.

Athickal, Joseph. *Maram Nagas: A Socio-Cultural Study.* New Delhi: Mittal Publications, 1992.

Athyal, Abraham P. and Dorothy Yoder Nyce. *Mission Today: Challenges and Concerns.* Chennai: Mission, Ecumenism & Dialogue Department Gurukhul Lutheran Theological College, 1998.

Athyal, Jesudas M., ed. *Mission Today Subaltern Perspectives: Mission-Evangelism Studies, Vol. II.* Thiruvalla: Christava Sahitya Samithi, 2001.

Athyal, Jesudas M., ed. *Relevant Patterns of Christian Witness in India; People as Agents of Mission, Mission – Evangelism Studies, Vol. I.* Thiruvalla: Christava Sahithya Samithy and Mission-Evangelism Study Project, 2000.

Athyal, Jesudas M., ed. *The Community we Seek Perspective on Mission*. Thiruvalla: Christian Sahitya Samithi, 2003.

Bareh, H., ed. *Gazetter of India-Nagaland: Kohima District.* Kohima: Government of Nagaland, 1970.

Bosch, David J. *Transforming Mission: Paradigm Shifts in Theology of Mission.* Maryknoll, New York: Orbis Books, 1996.

Das, S. T. *Tribal Life in North East India.* Delhi: Gian Publishing House, 1986.

Downs, F. S. *The Mighty Works of God: A Brief History of the Council of Baptist Churches in NEI: The Mission Period 1836-1950.* Guwahati: CLC, 1971.

Downs, F. S. *History of Christianity in India, Vol. 1, Part 5.* Bangalore: CHAI, 1992.

Dozo, Phuveyi. *The Cross over Nagaland.* Guwahati: CLC, 1983.

Elwin, Verrier. *Nagaland.* Shillong: P. Dutta for Research Department, 1961.

Elwin, Verrier. *The Nagas in the Nineteen Century.* London: Oxford University Press, 1969.

Epao, V. *From Naga Animism to Christianity.* New Delhi: Sanjivan Press, 1993.

From Darkness to Light: A Publication of the NBCC on the Occasion of the Celebration of 125 years of Christianity in Nagaland. Kohima: NBCC, 1997.

Hedlund, Roger E. *God and the Nations: A Biblical Theology of Mission in the Asian Context.* Delhi: ISPCK, 1997.

Hedlund, Roger E. and Paul Joshua Bhakiaraj, eds. *Missiology for the 21st Century: South Asian Perspective.* Delhi: ISPCK/MIIS, 2004.

Hiebert, Paul G. *Anthropological Insights for Missionaries.* Grand Rapids, Michigan: Baker Book House, 1998.

Horam, M. *North East India: A Profile.* New Delhi: Cosmo Publications, 1990.

Horam, M. *Social and Cultural Life of Naga: The Thangkhul Nagas.* Delhi: B. R. Publishing Corporation, 1977.

Horam, M. *Nagas Old Way New Trends.* New Delhi: Cosmo Publications, 1988.

Hussain, M. *Nagaland, Encyclopedia of India, Vol. XIX.* New Delhi: Rima Publishing House, 1994.

Irangbe, Heisuiding & Teiheilung Kulimbe. *Benreu Paupai Rennet Ha Laisiukwak.* Dimapur: Paupai Renet me Nkwah Benreu, 2004.

Jacobs, Julian. *The Nagas: Hill Peoples of Northeast India.* London: Thames and Hudson Ltd., 1990.

Jajo, Champhang. *Christian Life in a Tribal Context: in Manipur.* Calcutta: C. Jajo, 1990.

Jeganathan, W.S. Milton. *Mission Paradigm in the New Millennium.* Delhi: ISPCK, 2001.

Kanagaraj, Jey J. ed. *Mission & Missions: Essays in Honour of I. Ben Wati,* Pune: Union Biblical Seminary, 1998.

Kane, J. Herbert. *Winds of Change in the Christian Mission.* Chicago: Moody Press, 1973.

Kane, J. Herbert. *Understanding Christian Mission.* Grand Rapids, Michigan: Baker Book House, 1974.

Keitzar, Renthy. ed. *Good News for North East India: A Theological Reader.* Guwahati: CLC, 1995.

Keitzar, Renthy. *In Search of Relevant Gospel Message.* Guwahati: CLC, 1995.

Kipgen, M. *Christianity and Mizo Culture.* Aizawl: Mizo Theological Conference, 1996.

Kirk, J. Andrew. *What is Mission? Theological Explorations.* London: Darton, Longman and Todd Ltd., 1999.

Lindsell, Harold. *Missionary Principles and Practices.* West Wood, New Jersey: Fleming H. Revell Company, 1954.

Longchar, A. Wati. ed. *Encounter Between Gospel and Culture.* Jorhat: TSC. ETC, 1999.

Longchar, A. Wati. *The Traditional Tribal Worldview and Modernity: Focus on North East India.* Jorhat: N. Limala Lkr. Eastern Theological College, 1995.

Longchar, A. Wati. *The Tribal Religious Traditions in North East India: An Introduction,* Revised ed. Jorhat: Published by the Author, 2000.

Longchar, A. Wati. ed. *An Exploration of Tribal Theology*. Jorhat: Tzüdikong Baptist Church for the Tribal Study Centre, 1997.

Lotsüro, Angeline. *The Nagas: A Missionary Challenge.* Shillong: Vendrame Institute Publications, 2000.

Luzbetak, L. J. *The Church and Culture*: *New Perspectives in Missiological Anthropology.* Maryknoll: Orbis Books, 1988.

Mackenzie, A. *The North-East Frontier of India.* Delhi: Mittal Publications, 1989.

Makuga, G. *Introduction to the Rongmei Nagas.* Imphal: Mr & Mrs Makuga, 1994.

Mathew, C. V. Ed. *Mission in Context: Missiological Reflections Essays in Honour of Roger and June Hedlund.* Delhi: DMIIS/ISPCK, 2003.

Mattam, Joseph and Sebastian Kim, *Dimensions of Mission in India.* Bombay: St. Paul's Publication, 1995.

Monteiro, Evelyn. *Church and Culture: Communion in Pluralism.* Delhi: ISPCK, 2004.

Naga Institute of Culture (NIC) *A Brief Historical Account of Nagaland.* Kohima: 1970.

Namthiurei, M. P. *The Great Awakening.* Tamenglong: Golden Jubilee Publication, 1972.

Niebuhr, H. Richard. *Christ and Culture.* New York: Harper & Row, Publishers, 1951.

Pakem, B. *Coalition Politics in North East India.* New Delhi: Regency Publications, 1999.

Pamei, Namthiubuiyang. *The Trial from Makuilongdi: The Continuing Saga of the Zeliangrong People.* Tamenglong: Gironta Charitable Foundation, 2001.

Pamei, Ramkhun. *The Zeliangrong Nagas: A Sudy of Tribal Christianity.* New Delhi: Uppal Publishing House, 1996.

Perspectives on World Mission South Asia Versions. Bangalore: New Life Literature, 1998.

Philip, Puthuvail Thomas. *The Growth of Baptist Churches in Nagaland,* Guwahati: Christian Literature Centre, 1983 (Second edition).

Ponraj, S. D. *Missionary Anthropology: An Introduction.* Chennai: Mission Educational Books, 2004.

Presbyterian Church of India, *Manual of Worship*. Shillong: PCI, 2002.

Ramunny, Murkut. *The world of Nagas.* 2nd ed. New Delhi: Northern book centre, 1993.

Reid, Robert. *History of the Frontier Areas Bordering of Assam, 1883-1941*.Delhi: Eastern Publishing House, First Publish, 1942.

Sangma, Milton S. *History of American Baptist Mission in North East India (1836-1950)* Vol. 1. Delhi: Mittal Publications, 1987.

Scherer, James A. and Stephen B. Bevans, eds. *New Directions in Mission and Evangelization 1*. Maryknoll, New York: Orbis Books, 1998.

Sen, Sipra. *The Tribes and Castes of Manipur.* New Delhi: Mittal Publications, 1992.

Shimray, R. R. *Origin and Culture of Nagas.* New Delhi: Pamleiphi, 1985.

Singh, K. S. ed. *People of India-Nagaland,* Vol. XXXIV. Calcutta: Naveen Kishore, 1994.

Singh, K. S. ed. *Tribal Movement in India,* Vol. I. New Delhi: Manohar Publications, 1982.

Singh, K. S. ed. *Tribal Situation in India.* Shimla: Indian Institute of Advanced Study, 1972.

Song, C.S. *Third-Eye Theology*. New York: Orbis Book, 1979.

Stott, John R. W. *Christian Mission in the Modern World.* Bombay: Gospel Literature Service, 4th Reprint, 1993.

Suitei, comp. *Zeme Baptist Church Council (N): Pe reha, petah nah pe macet-mariam.* Peren Town: Published by the Compiler, 2002.

Takatemjen. *Studies on Theology and Naga Culture.* Jorhat: CTC, Aolijen, Mokokchung, 1997.

Thanzauva, K. *Theology of Community: Tribal Theology in the Making.* Aizawl: Mizo Theological Conference, 1997.

Thong, Joseph S. *Head-hunters Culture: Historic Culture of Nagas.* Chunlika Tsemenyu: Khinyi Woch, 1997.

Tylor, E. *Primitive Culture, Researches into the Development of Mythology, Phylosophy, Religion, Art and Custom.* London, 1871.

Verkuyl, J. *Contemporary Missiology: An Introduction.* William B. Eerdmans, 1987.

Verstraelen, F. J. *et al.* eds. *Missiology: An Ecumenical Introduction; Text and Context of Global Christianity.* Michigan: William B. Eerdmans Publishing Company, 1995.

Winter, Ralph D. and Steven C. Hawthorne, eds. *Perspective on the World Christian Movement: A Reader.* 3rd ed. Pasadena, California: William Carey Library, 1999.

Yonuo, Asoso. *The Rising Nagas: A Historical and Political Study.* Delhi: Vivek Publishing House, 1974.

Zeliang, Elungkiebe. *Charismatic Movements in the Baptist Churches in North East India: A Zeliangrong Perspective.* Delhi: ISPCK, 2014.

Unpublished materials

Gonmei, Rajen. "A Study of the Heraka Movement on the Socio, Political and Religious life of the Zeliangrong." B.D. thesis, Senate of Serampore College, 1994.

Haisuitei, "A Historical study of Christianity and Heraka (kampai cult) among the Zeliangrong People of Nagaland." B.D. thesis, Senate of Serampore College, 1989.

Hekwet, Rampaukube. "Analytical Study of the Zeliangrong Naga Traditional Ethical Values and Its implications for a Just Society." B.D. thesis, Senate of Serampore College, 2004.

Kauring, Iringtie."Rites and Rituals of the Zeliangrong Nagas and its Continuing Influence upon the Christians." B.D. thesis, Senate of Serampore College, 1999.

Kiphuina. "A Study on the Impacts of Revival Movements among the Zeliangrong Naga." B.D. thesis, Senate of Serampore College, 2006.

Nsa, Ramdeu. "Historical Study of Zeme Baptist Church Council (Nagaland)." B. D. thesis, Senate of Serampore College, 2003.

Zeliang, Elungkiebe. "The Socio-Economic and Political History of Zeliangrong Naga." B.D. thesis, Senate of Serampore College, 1996.

Zeliangrong Students Union Assam Manipur and Nagaland, Manuscript prepared for Publication (ZSU AMN), NP.

Souvenirs

Benreu Baptist Church Diamond Jubilee Souvenir. Benreu: 1981.

Benreu Baptist Church Centenary Celebration Committee Souvenir. Benreu: 1997.

Compendium: The Baptist Church of Mizoram, in Honor of BMS Mission in Mizoram 1903-2003. Serkawn: The Centenary Committee Baptist Church of Mizoram, 2003.

Nagaland Celebrates Quasqui Centennial: From Darkness to Light. Kohima: NBCC, 1997.

North East India Zeliangrong Naga Festival-Cum Seminar. Imphal: Literature and Sovenir Committee. NEIZNFS, 1995.

Peren District, Profile in Commemoration of Peren District Inauguration, 11th February, 2004.

Rongmei Baptist Church Burma Camp, *Silver Jubilee 1978-2003 Souvenir.* Dimapur: RBCBC, 2003.

The 4th Youth Conference RNBA. Tamenglong: RNBA Youth Department, 2003.

Zeliangrong Baptist Association Nagaland Silver Jubilee 1954-1979. Peren: ZBAN Silver Jubilee Souvenir Committee, 1979.

Zeliangrong Heraka Association Assam Nagaland Manipur. Tening: Zeliangrong Heraka Association, 2000.

Tingkao Ragwang Kalum Kai. Chingmeirong, Imphal: Zeliangrong Ra Chap-Riak Phom, 2001.

Interviews

Aniu. Deacon Samziuram Baptist Church. Interview, 18 October 2008.

Brother in charge. Pentecostal Church Jalukie Town. Interview, 18 October 2008.

Chewang, Kitanwi. ES, LBA Tening. Telephone interview, 4 April 2018.

Chirailule. Grant daughter of Mr. Songha (L) Jalukie Town. Interview, 19th November 2008.

Hedungziube. Leader of Heraka cult, Ziumi. Interview, 3 January 2008.

Hegui, Hiakie. Field Evangelist ZBCC, Peren. Interview, 1 November 2008.

Heigumchube. A member of Seventh Day Adventist Church Peren Town. Interview, 19 October 2008.

Hiapierai. Mission Secretary ZBCC, Peren Town. Interview, 28 January, 2009.

Ihecing. Evanglist of Northern Zeme Area Gaili. Interview, 14 October 2008.

Ileuheing. Field Evangelist, ZBCC. Interview, 27 December 2008.

Izieteilung. Executive Secretary, ZBCC. Telephone interview, 9 April 2018.

Kauring, Hialung. Retired government servant, Peren Town. Interview, 19 November 2008.

Kerugai. Pastor Samziuram Baptist Church. Interview, 18 October 2008.

Kupwa, D. Acting Pastor, Zeme Church Peren Town. Interview, 19 October 2008.

Kusa. Evangelist of Northern Zeme Area, Ngwalwa Town. Interview, 15 October 2008.

Kwetranglu. Pastor Azailong Baptist Church. Interview 11 October 2008.

Mariam, Aninge. Headmistress Zeliangrong Heraka School Tening. Interview, 16 October, 2008.

Mathiuthai. Executive Secretary, RBA. Telephone interview, 5 April 2018.

Mirhu. President Zeliangrong Students Union, AMN. Interview, 11 January 2009.

Ngimrai. Ordained Pastor Jalukie 'B' Baptist Church. Interview, 31st December 2008.

Nsa, Deuhing. Ordained minister ZBCC, Peren Town. Interview, 10 January 2009.

Nza, Peida. A member of prayer group Peren Town. Interview, 9 September 2008.

Nsa, Ramdeu. Mission Secretary, ZBCC. Telephone interview, 9 April 2018.

Pame, Cilak. President Zeme Theological Association North East India, Jalukie Town. Interview, 4 January 2009.

Pame, Rabi. Chairman Ordination Committee ZBA-J and Principal, UCTM Dimapur. Telephone interview, 4 April 2018.

Pame, Suigong. A Government School Teacher, Peren Town. Interview. 9 March 2009.

Ramdinthara. Ordained minister of the PCM also a M.Th. (New Testament) Second year student, ATC. Interview, 21 February 2009.

Rentta, Kamwang. Executive secretary and ordained minister of LBA. Tening Town. Interview, 16 October 2009.

Sahingmak. Executive Secretary, ZBA-J. Telephone interview, 5 April 2018.

Stephen. Chairman Presbyterian Church of North East India Samziuram. Interview, 18 October 2008.

Teubei. Former ES, ZBA Nsong. Telephone interview, 3 April 2018.

Thou, Kuzierang. Executive Secretary and an ordained minister of ZBCC, Peren Town. Interview, 9 October 2008.

Tunchapbo. A Theological Student from LBA, ATC, Aizawl. Interview, 27 January 2009.

Vechilhu. Prayer Chairman Christian Revival Prayer House Jalukie. Interview, 18 October 2008.

Reports

Annual Reports of the Council of Baptist Churches North East India. Guwahati. 1966.

Hiakie Hegui. Mission Secretary ZBCC Report. Presented at 57th Annual Session held at Zeme Baptist Church Dimapur. 18-20 January, 2008.

Kuzierang Thou. Executive Secretary ZBCC Report. Presented at 71st Annual Session NBCC. Kiusor. 1-3 February 2008.

Kamwang Rentta. Executive Secretary Report LBA. Presented at 71st Annual Session NBCC. Kiusor. 1-3 February 2008.

Pamphlets

Rongmei Baptist Association Nagaland, *"The 20th Foundation Day"* May 5, 2008.

Rongmei Baptist Association Nagaland, *Peoples Integrated Development Services*. Nd.

Constitutions

Constitution of the Zeliangrong Baptist Church Council, 24th January 1982.

Constitution of the Liangmai Baptist Association. Nd.

Others

ZBCC Samlia, Vol. 6, (September, 2008).

ZBCC Samlia, Vol. 5 (August, 2008).

ZBCC Samlia, Vol. 2 (September & October, 2008).

Zerang Lei. Peren: ZBCC Literature Committee. nd.

Zeliang, Elungkiebe. "A Reflection on Christmas Celebrations among the Tribal Christians of North East India."*Journal of Tribal Studies* 8/2 (July-December, 2004): 1-14.

Haraguchi, Takaaki. "Reflections on H. Richard Niebuhr's Theoretical Model Concerning the Relationship between Christianity and Culture: Its Applicability to the Japanese Context,"*Asia Journal of Theology* 21/ 2 (October 2007), 234.